Opening up
Psalms

ROGER ELLSWORTH

DayOne

Opening up
Psalms

ROGER ELLSWORTH

'Roger Ellsworth has given a very unique look at Psalms. He has exposed the reader to the great themes in a style easy to read, while mining deep theology. The book gives attention to the academic's need for rational explanation, but its most serious attention is to the revelation of God in the Spirit inspired hymnology. It makes for a valuable resource for the pastor looking for fresh insights, and for the layman who hungers to know God through the prism of human struggle. It was out of the human struggle the hymns came to us. Though the book does not touch on every Psalm, it shows the way to think through the imagery of the ancient hymns, and to enjoy their beauty.'

Jim Dixon
Pastor of First Baptist Church, Catalina, Arizona

'How does one say so much about the Psalms so briefly? Roger Ellsworth has done it! His categorizing of the Psalms is most helpful for new believers as well as experienced biblical scholars. I've had the joy of discovering Christ in the pages and have been convinced to be much occupied with God, to praise him more and to have greater faith in him. The book is brief enough for the busy theologian, deep enough to assist in sound exegesis, and stimulating enough to deepen the spiritual walk of ardent biblical scholars. I will most certainly recommend it for our seminary students. This book will most definitely serve the Christian church for the years to come and will have a prominent place on my own shelf.'

Nicki Coertze
Pastor of Christ Baptist Church and President of Christ Seminary, Polokwane, South Africa

© Day One Publications 2006

First printed 2006

All Scripture quotations, unless otherwise indicated, are taken from
the **New King James Version**®. Copyright © 1982 by Thomas Nelson, Inc.
Used by permission. All rights reserved.

ISBN 1 84625 005 -6

9 781846 250057

British Library Cataloguing in Publication Data available

Published by Day One Publications
Ryelands Road, Leominster, HR6 8NZ
Telephone 01568 613 740   FAX 01568 611 473

email—sales@dayone.co.uk
web site—www.dayone.co.uk
North American—e-mail-sales@dayonebookstore.com
North American web site—www.dayonebookstore.com

All rights reserved
No part of this publication may be reproduced, or stored in a retrieval system, or
transmitted, in any form or by any means, mechanical, electronic, photocopying,
recording or otherwise, without the prior permission of Day One Publications.

Designed by Steve Devane and printed by Gutenberg Press, Malta

The following pages are dedicated to my friends,
Ron, René, Adam, Sarah and Aaron Trotter

List of Bible abbreviations

THE OLD TESTAMENT		1 Chr.	1 Chronicles	Dan.	Daniel
		2 Chr.	2 Chronicles	Hosea	Hosea
Gen.	Genesis	Ezra	Ezra	Joel	Joel
Exod.	Exodus	Neh.	Nehemiah	Amos	Amos
Lev.	Leviticus	Esth.	Esther	Obad.	Obadiah
Num.	Numbers	Job	Job	Jonah	Jonah
Deut.	Deuteronomy	Ps.	Psalms	Micah	Micah
Josh.	Joshua	Prov.	Proverbs	Nahum	Nahum
Judg.	Judges	Eccles.	Ecclesiastes	Hab.	Habakkuk
Ruth	Ruth	S.of.S.	Song of Solomon	Zeph.	Zephaniah
1 Sam.	1 Samuel	Isa.	Isaiah	Hag.	Haggai
2 Sam.	2 Samuel	Jer.	Jeremiah	Zech.	Zechariah
1 Kings	1 Kings	Lam.	Lamentations	Mal.	Malachi
2 Kings	2 Kings	Ezek.	Ezekiel		

THE NEW TESTAMENT		Gal.	Galatians	Heb.	Hebrews
		Eph.	Ephesians	James	James
Matt.	Matthew	Phil.	Philippians	1 Peter	1 Peter
Mark	Mark	Col.	Colossians	2 Peter	2 Peter
Luke	Luke	1 Thes.	1 Thessalonians	1 John	1 John
John	John	2 Thes.	2 Thessalonians	2 John	2 John
Acts	Acts	1 Tim.	1 Timothy	3 John	3 John
Rom.	Romans	2 Tim.	2 Timothy	Jude	Jude
1 Cor.	1 Corinthians	Titus	Titus	Rev.	Revelation
2 Cor.	2 Corinthians	Philem.	Philemon		

Background and summary

The title

The name 'Psalms' means 'songs to the accompaniment of a stringed instrument'. It is taken from the Greek translation of the Old Testament, which used the title 'Psalmoi'. The Hebrew title for the book was 'Tehillim', which means 'praise songs'.

Authorship

The psalms were composed over a period of approximately 900 years, with the earliest being written by Moses (Ps. 90) and the latest written by various author after the Babylonian Captivity (e.g. Ps. 126; 147).

The psalms are primarily associated with David because he wrote most of them as the following breakdown indicates:

DAVID-73 (3-9; 11-32; 34-41; 41-65; 68-70; 86; 101; 103; 108-110; 122; 124; 131; 133; 138-145)

ASAPH-12 (50; 73-83)

DESCENDANTS OF KORAH-10 (42; 44-49; 84-85; 87)

SOLOMON-2 (72; 127)

ETHAN-1 (89)

HEMAN-1 (88)

MOSES-1 (90)

ANONYMOUS-50 (Many of these may also have been written by David. For example, Acts 4:25 attributes Psalm 2 to David.)

Divisions

The psalms fall into five 'books':

BOOK I-1-41 (41 psalms)
BOOK II-42-72 (31 psalms)
BOOK III-73-89 (17 psalms)
BOOK IV-90-106 (17 psalms)
BOOK V-107-150 (44 psalms)

Each of these 'books' ends with an emphatic and triumphant burst of praise (41:13; 72:18-19; 89:52; 106:48; 150:6).

Some have suggested that each corresponds thematically to the first five books of the Bible—the books of Moses. Because Book I emphasizes the themes of creation, sin and salvation, it supposedly corresponds to Genesis which prominently displays those same themes. Furthermore, because the psalms of Book II are weighted with the theme of redemption, it is said to correspond to the Book of Exodus.

This arrangement connects Book III with Leviticus because of their common emphasis on the sanctuary, Book IV with Numbers because of the prominence in each of Moses and Israel's wandering in the wilderness and Book V with Deuteronomy because of the emphasis in each on the Word of God.

This arrangement has the appearance of having been carried into the psalms instead of having been carried out of them. How easy it is to fall in love with some sort of scheme that comes to mind and then try to make the Scriptures fit!

Superscriptions

A good number of the psalms—116 to be exact—include either a historical or musical heading. The former gives us the situation in which the psalmist found himself when he sat down to write. The first of these is Psalm 3, which says, 'A Psalm of David when he fled from Absalom his son.' The latter gives instructions on how the psalm was to be played. The first musical heading is found in Psalm 4: 'To the Chief Musician. With stringed instruments. A Psalm of David.'

Selah Psalms

The word 'Selah' appears seventy-four times in forty psalms. This word signifies a pause or interlude. It may have been used to inform musicians to change instruments or to call for both musicians and listeners to ponder the truth that had been sung. In the public reading of the psalms, we honour each 'Selah', not by actually saying the word, but rather by pausing.

Types of poetry

The psalms display primarily three types of poetry. Synonymous parallelism is on display when the second line of a poem uses similar words to express the same thought as the first line. An example of this is:

O LORD, do not rebuke me in your anger,

Nor chasten me in your hot displeasure

(6:1).

Antithetical parallelism takes us to the other end of the

spectrum. Here the second line expresses the opposite of the first:

> The wicked borrows and does not repay,
>
> But the righteous shows mercy and gives
>
> (37:21).

Synthetic parallelism occurs when the second line carries further or expands the first line:

> God is our refuge and strength,
>
> A very present help in trouble
>
> (46:1).

Ascending parallelism takes place when succeeding lines repeat some words from the first line and complete the thought:

> Our fathers trusted in you;
>
> They trusted, and you
>
> delivered them.
>
> They cried to you, and were
>
> delivered;
>
> They trusted in you, and were
>
> not ashamed.
>
> (22:4-5).

Introduction

Our need for the psalms

Why should we concern ourselves with the Book of Psalms? Yes, it is the longest book in the Bible—much longer than its closest competitor, Isaiah. It is the only book of the Bible that was written by many authors. It contains both the longest and shortest chapters of the Bible, 119 and 117 respectively. It is the Old Testament book most frequently quoted by New Testament writers. It contains much by way of soothing language.

These are some of the features that lend interest and fascination to the book, but its true significance lies in its timeless message.

And what is its message? The Book of Psalms, as is the case with every other book of the Bible, is a message about the Lord Jesus Christ. We must find the Lord Jesus here because he found himself here. As he walked with two of his disciples on the day of his resurrection, Jesus 'expounded to them in all the Scriptures the things concerning himself' (Luke 24:27).

Later that day he appeared to other disciples and said: 'These are the words which I spoke to you while I was still with you, that all things must be fulfilled which were written in the Law of Moses and the Prophets and the Psalms concerning Me' (Luke 24:44).

> All of Scripture is about the Lord Jesus Christ and his redeeming work, and that includes the psalms!

All of Scripture is about the Lord Jesus Christ and his redeeming work, and that includes the psalms!

But where do we find him in the psalms? In prophecy! There are more prophecies of Christ in the psalms than any other book of the Old Testament! Some of these, as we shall see, are so very detailed and precise that they appear to be the descriptions of those actually viewing the events instead of foretelling them hundreds of years before.

The Open Bible [1] gives the following helpful list of specific messianic references in the psalms:

Prophecy	Fulfilment
2:7 God will declare him to be his Son.	Matt. 3:17
8:6 All things will be put under his feet.	Hebrews 2:8
16:10 He will be resurrected from the dead.	Mark 16:6,7
22:1 God will forsake him in his hour of need.	Matt. 27:46
22:7,8 He will be scorned and mocked.	Luke 23:35
22:16 His hands and feet will be pierced.	John 20:25,27
22:18 Others will gamble for his clothes.	Matt. 27:35,36
34:20 Not one of his bones will be broken.	John 19:32,33,36
35:11 He will be accused by false witnesses.	Mark 14:57
35:19 He will be hated without a cause.	John 15:25
40:7,8 He will come to do God's will.	Hebrews 10:7
41:9 He will be betrayed by a friend.	Luke 22:47
45:6 His throne will be forever.	Hebrews 1:8

68:18 He will ascend to God's right hand.	Mark 16:19
69:9 Zeal for God's house will consume him.	John 2:17
69:21 He will be given vinegar and gall to drink.	Matt. 27:34
109:4 He will pray for his enemies.	Luke 23:34
109:8 His betrayer's office will be filled by another.	Acts 1:20
110:1 His enemies will be made subject to him.	Matt.22:44
110:4 He will be a priest like Melchizedek.	Hebrews 5:6
118:22 He will be the chief cornerstone.	Matt. 21:42
118:26 He will come in the name of the Lord.	Matt. 21:91

We need the psalms, then, because they point us to Christ, who is the source of our salvation. But we also need them because they describe the life of the saved-that is, the qualities that those who have faith in Christ are to seek and to practise. More specifically, the psalms:

TEACH US TO BE MUCH OCCUPIED WITH GOD. They magnify and exalt him as the Sovereign Creator and Ruler of the universe. What is it to be much occupied with God? It is ' … to treasure his Word, to delight in his worship, to reflect on his glorious attributes, to rehearse his great acts in history, to trust in his care, to glory in his gospel and to anticipate his final victory. The more occupied with God we are, the more strength we find for living.'[2]

TEACH US TO PRAISE GOD and show us how to praise him. There are few lessons that we more need. So very often we mumble mechanical praise from hearts that are crowded with unworthy loves and occupied with earthly concerns. The need is for robust praise from hearts that are deeply schooled in the stunning truths of the Sovereign Lord who not only made us but pours from his bounty countless blessings, the chief of which is eternal salvation through his Son.

TEACH US TO HAVE FAITH IN GOD in our afflictions and to receive comfort from him. They express every human emotion and address every human need. John R. W. Stott writes: 'The reason why Christian people are drawn to the psalms is that they speak the universal language of the human soul... Whatever our spiritual mood may be, there is sure to be a psalm which reflects it—whether triumph or defeat, excitement or depression, joy or sorrow, praise or penitence, wonder or anger.'3

> We might say the psalms show us how to respond to every conceivable situation that life throws at us.

We might say the psalms show us how to respond to every conceivable situation that life throws at us. William Hendriksen notes: 'In the psalms the believer pours out his heart before Jehovah. Accordingly, expressions of repentance, communion, hope, faith, love, etc., abound. There are psalms for every occasion in life and for every spiritual condition, so that the Psalter is universal in its appeal to believing hearts.'4

TEACH US TO HAVE ZEAL FOR GOD'S CAUSE. From hearts flooded with love for God, the various psalmists expressed fervent desires to see the advancement of God's truth, the vindication of his name, the acknowledgement of his glory and the triumph of his kingdom.

All of this requires, as the imprecatory psalms so wonderfully comprehend, the defeat of evil and the judgement of evil-doers.

Such zeal for God constitutes a stinging rebuke to all those professing believers who have been afflicted with 'spectatoritis'. This malady turns people into mere church-goers who attend to get some kind of 'fix'—a little shot of something to make them feel good about themselves, all, of course, laced with lots of fun and humour.

TEACH US TO VALUE AND PRACTISE both public worship and private devotion. The psalms throb with both kinds of worship. The former is vigorously endorsed in the pilgrimage psalms, as well as in other types. And the latter is modelled by individual psalmists who, even in the midst of heart-wrenching circumstances, find their hearts going out after God in praise and adoration.

Method of study

The sheer magnitude of the psalms makes it impossible in a commentary of this nature to do a psalm-by-psalm exposition. How do we, then, go about this matter of 'opening up' the psalms? I propose that we do a category-by-category study. In each category we will take a quick look, a closer look and an even closer look. The 'quick look' will amount to little more than a list of the major psalms in that category. The 'closer look' will consist of a summary or overview of one, two or three of the psalms. The 'even closer look' will feature a more in-depth exposition of one psalm in that category.

The purpose of the following pages is not, therefore, to be exhaustive but suggestive. It is to tantalize, to make the reader want to go deeper into the psalms. My favourite

Mexican restaurant offers a 'sampler platter', as does my favourite seafood restaurant. What follows is a 'sampler platter' from the psalms. Or, to change the figure, a sight-seeing tour that will take us to some but not all of the major sights.

Types of psalms

The approach I am proposing is not without difficulties. One problem is that there is little agreement among Bible scholars on the various types of psalms. Some see eight categories, while others see nine or ten or more.

> I invite you, then, to join me on a sight-seeing journey through the Psalms. It must of necessity be brief. There is so much that we will not be able to see!

Another problem is that some psalms fit into more than one category. An example of this is Psalm 40 which has been classified as a psalm of individual lament, individual thanksgiving and imprecatory. A few of the pilgrimage psalms—127; 128; 133—are placed by some in the 'wisdom' category. Still others of those psalms—125; 131—are placed by some in the 'confidence' category.

David M. Fleming observes: 'Clear-cut categorization is not possible for every psalm, nor does every psalm fit a particular category. ...A reader of the Psalms will find that different psalms can be grouped by similarities of form, content, and pattern. Yet, variations do occur, and each psalm is unique in both message and content.'[5]

While categorization must of necessity be imprecise, it is still helpful. I propose, therefore, that we look at the following types: wisdom, confidence, individual laments, communal laments, pilgrimage, individual thanksgiving, communal thanksgiving, general praise, descriptive praise, imprecatory, indirectly messianic, explicitly messianic, enthronement.

I invite you, then, to join me on a sight-seeing journey through the Psalms. It must of necessity be brief. There is so much that we will not be able to see! But those sights which we do see will certainly make the journey worthwhile. By the way, this journey requires, as all journeys do, a suitcase packed with the proper items. So be sure to bring a mind that is ready to ponder the glories of God and a heart that is ready to stand in awe of them.

1 Wisdom psalms

A quick look

The wisdom psalms are those which offer the reader instruction and guidance for living righteously. David M. Fleming writes: 'Wisdom psalms probe life's mysteries to teach the congregation about itself and God.'[1]

As noted above, some regard certain pilgrimage psalms as also belonging to the wisdom category (127; 128; 133). While consensus is lacking, the following psalms are often placed in the 'wisdom' category: 1; 14; 37; 49; 53; 73; 78; 112; 119.

Of these, Psalms 1, 73 and 119 have been especially prized by the people of God.

A closer look

Psalm 73

Written by Asaph, a Levite musician appointed by David to serve in the tabernacle (1 Chron. 6:31-32,39), this psalm deals with a problem that is just as up to date as when it was written, namely, the problem of the wicked flourishing while the righteous languish.

THE PROSPERITY OF THE WICKED

Asaph says the wicked 'are not in trouble as other men; nor are they plagued like other men' (v. 5). It seemed to him that the wicked did not struggle in life. He says, 'They have more than heart could wish' (v. 7). And they did not even appear to struggle in death. Asaph notes that there were 'no pangs in their death; but their strength is firm' (v. 4).

Perhaps most disconcerting to Asaph was the attitude of the wicked in all of this. One would at least expect them to realize something of the degree of their blessing and to show a smidgen of gratitude and a dash of humility. But such was not the case. They showed no appreciation for their blessings and no concern for those around them who were not so blessed. Instead, they went about brandishing pride as though it were a chain about their necks (v. 6). Further, they did not hesitate to speak 'loftily' (v. 8). Instead of thanking God for their tranquillity and affluence, they 'set their mouth against the heavens' (v. 9).

THE DIFFICULTY OF THE RIGHTEOUS

Asaph would have been satisfied if he had been able to see the people of God doing as well as the wicked. But he says that they were drinking all day and each day out of a full cup of affliction (vv. 10,14).

Caught in the vice of the prosperity of the wicked and the adversity of the righteous, Asaph finally gave way to this melancholy cry of despair: 'Surely I have cleansed my heart in vain, and washed my hands in innocence' (v. 13). He had reached his lowest point.

THE WAY OF RELIEF

What Asaph refused to do

Asaph refused to infect the people of God with his doubt and despair (v. 15). By writing this psalm, Asaph finally shared his despair with all future generations of believers, but only after he had worked through it. We might say he refrained from writing when he had only the first fourteen verses to write. He took up his pen only when he had the last fourteen verses.

Our first conclusions regarding our problems are seldom our best, and if we quickly share those initial conclusions we may do considerable harm to the faith of others.

What Asaph did

Asaph says he 'went into the sanctuary of God' (v. 17). This was the decisive thing, the turning point, in this crisis. There he found what he needed.

What was there about the house of God that helped Asaph? Was it the public reading of the Word of God? Was it the exposition of that Word? Was it something he heard in his conversation with other believers? It could have been one or more of these things. The important thing is that the answer came to him while he was engaged in the public worship of God.

There in the Lord's house, Asaph realized he had been content to look solely at the here and now. He had failed to consider all the facts. When he went to public worship, he began to think in terms of eternity. (The house of the Lord does have a wonderful way of bringing the eternal to bear upon the temporal.)

As Asaph pondered the end of the wicked, he came to see that this is really the decisive thing. It is the end that makes the difference. It did not matter how happy and prosperous they appeared to be in this life. The immensely important matter was what lay ahead of them. Asaph began to understand that with all their care-free days and ways, the wicked were standing on a slippery slope and would ultimately be plunged into eternal destruction.

Asaph's experience should lead us to understand that the righteous on his worst day is far better off than the unrighteous on his best day.

Psalm 119

The writer, usually considered to be David, registers his delight in the Word of God in an unusual way. The psalm consists of twenty-two sections each of eight verses. Each of these twenty-two sections features a letter of the Hebrew alphabet. For instance, each of the eight verses in the first section begins with the Hebrew letter 'Aleph'. Each of the verses in the next section begins with the Hebrew letter 'Beth'. And so it goes through the entire Hebrew alphabet.

While this psalm deals with many aspects of the Word of God, two major themes emerge more forcefully than any others: why we should value the Word of God and how we show that we value the Word of God.

WHY WE SHOULD VALUE THE WORD OF GOD

The psalm gives two major answers to this inquiry. It first tells us we are to value God's Word…

Because of what it is

VARIOUS NAMES This psalm employs ten names for the Word of God: word, law, saying, statutes, way, commandments, path, testimonies, precepts, and judgements. A mere glance at these words is sufficient to realize that God's Word is more precious than words can convey. It is God himself speaking. It is God's law for our lives. It is God testifying of himself. It is God providing guidance for our walk in this world. All of these things and more are conveyed by these ten names.

VARIOUS PICTURES But the importance of the Word of God is also conveyed by several graphic pictures. The psalmist likens the Word of God to water (v. 9), a treasure, (vv. 14,72,127,162), a companion and counsellor (v. 24), a song (v. 54), honey (v. 103), light (vv. 105,130), and a heritage (v. 111).

How valuable are these things? What would life be like without them? They are only faint glimmers of the value of the Word of God!

The psalmist also tells us that we should value the Word of God…

Because of what it does

IT BRINGS HAPPINESS (vv. 1-2). The word 'blessed' means 'happy'. The psalmist is, therefore, asserting something of strategic importance—our happiness is tied to valuing the Word of God! Tragically, the devil has succeeded in convincing most that the opposite is true. They see God's commands as being detrimental to their happiness, but just the opposite is the case. The key to happiness is to live in God's Word and to let his Word live in us.

IT PRODUCES CLEANSING (vv. 9,11). The Word of God is the agent the Spirit of God used to regenerate the hearts of all of us who are saved (Eph. 5:25-27), and he continues to use that same cleansing power in our lives. By that Word, the Holy Spirit shows us what pleases God and what doesn't and, in so doing, calls us away from sin and into purity of life.

It is noteworthy that the psalmist specifically relates the cleansing power of the Word of God to young men (v. 9). He knew the tendency of young men to fall into unclean living, and he wanted them to understand that devotion to the Word of God could preserve them from such living.

IT GIVES LIBERTY (v. 45). Sin always promises to bring freedom, but it only creates bondage (2 Peter 2:19). It is the truth of God that brings true and lasting freedom (John 8:32).

IT PROVIDES DIRECTION (v. 105). We live in a dark, perplexing world that offers us many paths. If we are careless about the paths we choose, we invite misery and ruin. The Word of God provides the direction we need. It is like a light shining in a dark place (2 Peter 1:19).

IT PRODUCES UNDERSTANDING (v. 130). Our walking and understanding are inseparably linked. In addition to shedding light on our path, the Word of God enlightens our minds so we can discern what we ought to do.

HOW WE SHOW WE VALUE THE WORD OF GOD

A second major emphasis in this psalm is this: how we show that we value the Word of God.

Studying it
Firstly, we will study it diligently. God's purpose in giving his

Word was to point us to himself. We are, therefore, to seek him through his Word (v. 2), and this seeking is to be done wholeheartedly (vv. 2-10). We are to 'look' into his Word (v. 6) and to learn its judgements (v. 7).

> This means we are to store [God's Word] in our minds and treasure it in our affections with the confidence that it will fortify us against sin.

Obeying it

Secondly, we will obey its commands. The duty of obedience is set forth in these verses in several ways: walking in the law of the Lord and in his ways (vv. 1,3), keeping his testimonies (vv. 2,129), and taking heed to our ways to make sure they correspond to the teachings of God's Word (v. 9).

Storing it

Thirdly, we will hide it in our hearts. This means we are to store it in our minds and treasure it in our affections with the confidence that it will fortify us against sin (v. 11). G. Campbell Morgan summarizes this verse in this way: 'The best book, in the best place, for the best purpose.'[2]

Declaring it

Fourthly, we will declare it to others (v. 13). Studying the Word of God will cause our hearts to burn within us (Luke 24:32) in such a way that we won't be able to keep it to ourselves. We'll be anxious to share its message of salvation with those who don't know Christ and to discuss its teachings with fellow Christians.

Rejoicing over it

Finally, we will constantly rejoice over the Word of God and delight in it (vv. 14-16). We must not miss the connection the psalmist makes in these verses. The rejoicing of verse 14 and the delighting of verse 16 are connected by the meditating of verse 15. As we reflect on what the Word of God is and what it does, we will find the rejoicing and delighting to be inescapable.

FOR FURTHER STUDY

1. Read Matthew 7:13-14. What did Jesus teach about the differences between the righteous and the wicked?
2. Read Jeremiah 23:29, Hebrews 4:12 and James 1:21-25. What pictures are used in these verses for the Word of God?

TO THINK ABOUT AND DISCUSS

1. In what ways can you show esteem and appreciation for the house of God and the Word of God?
2. What is the proper way for Christians to respond to those who have no regard for God?

2 An even closer look: Psalm 1

The wisdom of the righteous

This psalm is a jewel. A favourite among the people of God down through the centuries, it earns its way into the wisdom category by presenting a powerful contrast between the righteous and the wicked.

It falls quite naturally into two parts: the blessedness of the godly (vv. 1-3) and the wretchedness of the ungodly (vv. 4-6). The psalmist considers the states of both in some detail.

The blessedness of the godly person (vv. 1-3)

The psalm begins with an exultant burst: 'Blessed is the man …' This amounts to the psalmist saying: 'How very happy is the man …'

It would seem to many that the author of this psalm was setting off on a fool's errand. Imagine it! The man intends to show that the person who devotes himself to living a godly and righteous life is the one who finds true happiness, while the one who lives without regard to God is the miserable person!

The world has it the other way. The God-devoted person is miserable! And those who live unshackled by thoughts of God find the fun!

Time will prove the psalmist to be correct.

The psalmist unfolds the happiness of the righteous along three lines.

What the godly person refuses (v. 1)

THE COUNSEL OF THE UNGODLY If we replace the word 'counsel' with the word 'advice', we quickly get to the nub of the matter. The righteous person does not govern his life on the basis of bad advice from bad people.

Ours is a time in which those who have no room for God are ever ready and eager to offer advice to those who are living for God. The advice of the godless is all around. It crops up in personal conversations, in magazine and newspaper articles, in movies and television shows. All of these—and others too—join their voices in the incessant, pounding cry: 'Live like this! It's fun! You'll be glad you did!'

The godly person does, from time to time, give heed to godless advice, but he always does so to his own hurt. The principle of spiritual life that has been placed within him will not allow unqualified and ongoing consent to such advice. The spiritual person will inevitably see that his wholeness is directly tied to his wholeheartedness. The more wholeheartedly he rejects evil advice, the more whole (in the sense of being happy) he will be.

THE PATH OF SINNERS The focus shifts from the advice offered by the godless to their lifestyle or pattern of behaviour. It is one which does not conform to the laws of God. Seeing this, the godly person avoids it. He does not stand in this path, lingering with those who tread it.

It is not contact with the godless that the godly seeks to avoid. It is rather camaraderie.

THE SEAT OF THE SCORNFUL Scornful people are those who hold nothing sacred, scoffing at God and all that is associated with him. To 'sit' with such people takes us a step further than walking and standing. It suggests remaining or abiding with them and enjoying their company.

The godly person always feels out of place and unhappy around those who make sport of God.

What the godly person chooses (v. 2)

The godly person finds happiness in 'the law of the LORD'. The word 'law' itself means 'teaching,' 'instruction' or 'direction'. We usually associate 'the law of the LORD' with the law God gave to Moses or with the books of Moses (the first five books of the Bible). But, as Psalm 119 makes clear, the term also refers to the whole truth of God as it is revealed in the Word of God. It is surely this broad sense that the author of Psalm 1 had in mind.

DELIGHTING IN GOD'S WORD The author has affirmed that the godly person does not take counsel from the wicked. Now he states it positively. The godly person takes his counsel from the Word of God. This Word is his delight. He finds it to be immensely interesting and relevant. It brings him joy and satisfaction.

What does it mean to delight in the Word of God? Here is a man who is in love with a woman. He delights in her. He yearns to spend time with her. And when he is with her, he drinks in every word she speaks. He is intoxicated with her beauty. So it is with the godly person and the Word of God!

MEDITATING ON GOD'S WORD The psalmist goes a step further. The godly person also meditates on the Word of God 'day and night'. The word 'meditate' means 'to murmur' or 'to mutter'. It means 'speaking to one's self in a low voice'.

> The word 'meditate' means 'to murmur' or 'to mutter'. It means 'speaking to one's self in a low voice'.

The Word of God is never far from the thoughts of the saint of God. When he is depressed or distressed, he calls to mind its promises. When he is uncertain and perplexed, he considers its guidelines. When his sins loom before him like evil spectres, he ponders its glorious proclamation of the love of God in and through Jesus Christ. He finds that the Word of God has a joy for every sorrow and a truth for every situation.

What the godly person realizes (v. 3)

The outcome of the godly person's refusing and choosing is not left in doubt. He will be 'like a tree'.

What does the tree suggest? Strength and stability! Fruitfulness! Beauty! Refreshing shade!

All of these things are found in the one who delights in the Word of God. And the degree of the delight is the degree to which they are found. The delighting person has strength and stability in the storms of life. He manifests the virtues and qualities that are called the fruit of the Spirit (Gal. 5:22-23). And such a life makes him beautiful and refreshing to others.

The prophet Jeremiah uses the same imagery of the believer as an unwithering, firmly rooted, flourishing tree.

But he speaks of the unbeliever as a shrub in the desert (Jer. 17:5-8). The choice placed before each of us is between shrub-living and tree-living. The difference lies in how we regard the Word of God.

Jesus himself drew the same distinction in terms of two builders. He likened those who refused to heed his word to one who built on sand and those who heeded his word to one who built on a rock. When the storm came, the house on the sand fell while the house on the rock stood firm (Matt. 7:24-27). The difference, again, was in the response to the Word of God.

The contrast drawn by Jeremiah and Jesus leads us to that drawn by the psalmist, as he turns to present—

The wretchedness of the ungodly person (vv. 4-6)

If anything, the difference between the godly and the ungodly is more powerfully presented by the psalmist than by Jeremiah. Chaff is even less substantial than a shrub!

The psalmist's mention of chaff takes us back to the farming techniques of that time. The farmer would place the wheat he had harvested on a stone threshing floor and drive his oxen around it so that their hooves would separate the grain from the husks. He would then use a kind of fork or shovel to pitch the grain and the chaff in the air. The grain would fall to the floor to be preserved and the chaff would be blown away.

The chaff represents those whose lives are not rooted in the Word of God.

The Bible tells us that a day of separation is coming. John the Baptist had this to say regarding the Lord Jesus Christ:

'His winnowing fan is in his hand, and he will thoroughly purge his threshing floor, and gather his wheat into the barn; but he will burn up the chaff with unquenchable fire' (Matt. 3:12).

The ungodly 'shall not stand' on that day of judgement. And they will have no place 'in the congregation of the righteous.' Those who choose to live apart from God and his people in this life will find that they will have no part with them in eternity. Those who stand with the ungodly in this life will not be able to stand with the righteous at that time.

Is there wisdom in this psalm? Indeed, there is. There is no greater wisdom than ordering our lives according to the Word of God. The central truth of that Word is the saving work of the Lord Jesus Christ, and the major part of that ordering lies in receiving that work.

FOR FURTHER STUDY

1. Read 2 Samuel 13. Who offered ungodly advice? Of what did it consist? Who received it? What were the results?
2. Read Revelation 20:11-15. What does this passage teach about the judgement of the wicked?

TO THINK ABOUT AND DISCUSS

1. Jot down some ways in which many are looking for happiness.
2. Identify some ways in which you find yourself pressured to engage in ungodly behaviour or to think in ungodly ways.

3 Confidence psalms

A quick look

These are psalms that express faith in God's care for and guidance of his people. Some examples are: 4; 11; 16; 23; 27; 62; 91; 125; 131. The last two are also known as 'Songs of Ascents', which we will have occasion to notice in the section entitled 'Pilgrimage psalms'.

A closer look

Psalm 4

Sometimes called 'The Evening Psalm', David here expresses trust in God that enabled him to sleep and rest even though he was in the midst of trying circumstances. The historical setting of this psalm is believed to be Absalom's rebellion against David (2 Sam. 15:1-18:33).

Steven J. Lawson writes of this psalm: 'Life should be lived with the assurance of God's sovereignty, knowing that he rules over everything for his glory. Even when it seems as if the ungodly have dominated the scene, believers should remember that God has chosen the godly for himself and will not forsake them. This is the central message of Psalm 4, a song that provides a Godward focus in the midst of life's storms.'[1]

The psalm consists of four major sections.

DAVID ADDRESSES THE LORD (V. 1)

In times of trouble David instinctively turned to prayer. Michael Wilcock explains: ' … the psalmist is convinced that prayer is a necessity. In his greatest distress … , prayer is his greatest resource. Even when he is blaming God, he still cries to God. Against all the odds, he is sure that there must still be an ultimate framework of right, upheld by the righteous God (v. 1), behind all the wrongs which God allows to happen.'[2]

DAVID ADDRESSES THE 'SONS OF MEN' (VV. 2-3)

This is the way in which David chose to address his enemies. He may very well have chosen this term to remind his enemies who were so filled with pride and so sure of themselves that they were nothing but mere clay!

These enemies, headed by his own son, took enormous pleasure in what they were doing, namely, taking the glorious kingdom of Israel away from David, undoubtedly assuring themselves that they would lead it to even greater glory.

What they thought they knew would prove to be false. There was no glory in what they were doing, only shame. And the thing they most needed to know was that David's reign was God-ordained and would not end until God said so.

DAVID ADDRESSES HIMSELF (VV. 4-5)

The rebellion of Absalom posed a stern challenge to David. How should he respond to such a blatant, arrogant attack? In these verses, he coaches himself. He must not let legitimate anger creep over the line into sinful anger. He must still himself before God and meditate on what he knows to be the truth of God. Furthermore, he must concentrate on doing right and put his trust in the Lord.

DAVID AGAIN ADDRESSES THE LORD (VV. 6-8)

Circumstances were such that it appeared to David's friends as if good had perished from the earth. But David, resorting again to prayer, would have none of this. He asked the Lord to smile upon him and his friends and to put gladness in their hearts. Knowing that the Lord was indeed capable of doing this, David could lie down in peace and sleep.

Psalm 11

Beginning with the words 'In the LORD I put my trust; ...,' David expresses confidence in God even though wickedness appeared to be so very strong. Steven J. Lawson writes: 'David was facing a national crisis that threatened to overturn the stability of the nation of Israel. All around him, the moral foundations of the people were crumbling. This upheaval was caused by evil men who sought to do him harm. Adding to this ordeal, the people who were loyal to David panicked, counselling him to flee Jerusalem. But David remained calm and resolute, keeping his eyes on the Lord. In this hour of crisis, David determined to trust in God in spite of his

> David expresses confidence in God even though wickedness appeared to be so very strong.

circumstances. His faith, unshakable and unwavering, kept him steadfast in uncertain times.'3

The psalm can be divided into two parts: the counsel of despair (vv. 1-3) and the response of faith (vv. 4-7). The first is the voice which David heard. The second is the voice with which he answered.

THE COUNSEL OF DESPAIR (VV. 1-3)

The psalm begins with a note of surprise. David was trusting in the Lord in the midst of his trial (v. 1). Although his faith was well known to his friends, this did not keep them from grimly advising him to 'Flee as a bird' (v. 2).

To them it was all very clear. The wicked were ready to shoot 'secretly' (v. 2)—from the cover of darkness—at the godly.

David's friends evidently considered his adversaries to be so numerous, so strong and so crafty that there was little hope of success against them. It appeared as if these enemies would cause the very foundations of society to be destroyed.

We often hear the same gloomy assessment that was given to David. Wickedness is so strong and flourishing! The foundations are crumbling! All is hopeless! The righteous can do nothing to stem the tide!

THE RESPONSE OF FAITH (VV. 4-7)

David's friends quite clearly expected one answer and one answer alone when they asked: 'What can the righteous do?' (v. 3). That answer was: nothing!

But David would have none of it! The very same logic offered to him on this occasion would have kept him from facing Goliath! David refused to yield to it then, and he here refuses it again. He does so for the very same reason, namely, his faith in God. The God who was greater than Goliath was also greater than the wicked who were seeking to destroy the foundations!

So David sets himself to remind his friends of certain key truths about God. He is sovereign over all (v. 4a). He is well aware of the wicked and what they are doing (v. 4b). He is not ambivalent about evil but has the utmost hatred for it and in due time will bring judgement on the wicked (vv. 5-6). Conversely, the Lord loves righteousness and smiles upon those who practise it (v. 7).

Such truths present us with a sharp dilemma. If the Lord indeed loves righteousness and hates evil, why does he allow evil to flourish and to trouble his people? David does not attempt a detailed answer. He wrote to affirm his faith, not to unravel the tangled thread of evil. But he does drop a hint for us: 'The Lord tests the righteous' (v. 5).

When evil thrives, it gives the people of God the opportunity to show the stuff of which they are made, to show that they do not love and serve God only in fair weather but also in foul.

Psalm 91

This psalm has long been a favourite of the people of God. Its opening verses are some of the best known and most quoted. It is not hard to see why this psalm is so loved. It is one of the most comforting in all the Bible. More specifically, it offers comfort for the fearful and troubled. Only those who have never been fearful and troubled can afford to neglect it.

The psalm may be structured around three speakers: the first speaker offers a general statement (v. 1), the psalmist responds (v. 2), the first speaker elaborates (vv. 3-13) and the Lord speaks (vv. 14-16).

THE GENERAL STATEMENT (V. 1)

Here the first speaker—or perhaps a choir—affirms the blessedness of the individual who 'dwells in the secret place of the Most High'. This suggests intimacy with the Almighty. God does not leave his child in the foyer but takes him into his special den. It is an indication of friendship.

THE RESPONSE (V. 2)

The psalmist determines that he will seek this wonderful blessing. He will make the Lord his refuge and fortress. He will trust in him.

THE ELABORATION (VV. 3-13)

The first speaker now assures the psalmist that his resolve will be rewarded with rich blessings. The Lord will either deliver him from or help him through some of life's most vexing and challenging problems. What troubles are depicted here! There are those calamities that suddenly and unexpectedly come upon us (the snare of the fowler—v. 3; lions and serpents—v. 13). There are pestilence-like dangers (v. 3), that is, those fears and

> The Lord will either deliver him from or help him through some of life's most vexing and challenging problems.

anxieties we pick up from those around us. The 'terror by night' (v. 5) may refer to those disconcerting and distressing thoughts that fly through our minds and rob us of sleep. Then there are those dangers that arise from the antagonism of others ('the arrow that flies by day'—v. 5). Arrows don't just fly. They have to be shot by someone. Add to these 'the pestilence that walks in darkness' (v. 6). This may very well refer to those dangers that strike when we think we are most safe—that is, at night when we have retired in what we consider to be the safety of our homes. 'The destruction that lays waste at noonday' (v. 6) may represent those calamities that arise when we are in our most productive years. Finally, there are those dangers we bring upon ourselves by being preoccupied and undiscerning. Stones (v. 12) don't strike or pounce, but they can inflict real hurt. How many hurt themselves by simply being careless and oblivious to the stones that lie in their path!

The Lord is more than sufficient for all of these. He delivers (v. 3) and covers or protects (v. 4). While others are dropping like flies (v. 7), the believer is safe. He only has to look at it (v. 8) and not actually experience it.

Some argue that the teachings of this psalm are simply not true. They think of someone who was not protected from or delivered from calamity and conclude on that basis that this psalm is mistaken. What are we to say about this? The following should be kept in mind:

1. Most of the time God does keep us from calamity. John Calvin says, 'When we look back on our life from the perspective of eternity, we are going to see that the power of Satan was so great, that the weakness of our flesh was feeble,

and that the hostility of the world was so strong, that every day of our lives—if God had not intervened—we would never have made it through a day.'4

2. Sometimes God allows calamities to come upon us for our good. Matthew Henry says: 'Though trouble or affliction befall thee, yet there shall be no real evil in it, for it shall come from the love of God and shall be sanctified; and it shall come, not for thy hurt, but for thy good; and though, for *the present, it be not joyous but grievous*, yet, in the end, it shall yield so well that thou thyself shall own *no evil befel thee*.'5

3. When God does allow something hurtful to come into our lives, he is there to strengthen us and to help us bear it.

THE WORD OF THE LORD (VV. 14-16)

The psalm concludes with the Lord assuring the psalmist that he does indeed deliver his people (v. 14), that he hears and answers their prayers (v. 15), that he blesses them with his presence (v. 15), satisfies them with long life (v. 16) and finally shows them his salvation (v. 16).

The promise of long life may cause some to question. Certainly there are many believers who die at a young age. But the promise probably underscores the fact that the qualities of a godly life are such that they are likely to yield long life and more satisfaction in life.

And let us never forget that all the promises that seem to fall short of fulfilment in this life will finally be perfectly fulfilled in that glorious eternal day of salvation.

For further study ▶

FOR FURTHER STUDY

1. Read 1 Samuel 17. In what ways did David express faith when Israel was confronted with Goliath?
2. Psalm 91:1-2 refers to God as both a shadow and a fortress. Find other passages in which God is described in these ways.

TO THINK ABOUT AND DISCUSS

1. Write down some ways in which you can improve your prayer life.
2. Talk with some friends about ways in which God has protected you.

4 An even closer look: Psalm 23

The twenty-third psalm is certainly the best loved of all the confidence psalms and probably the best loved of all Scriptures. David wrote it to express his confidence in the Lord's care for him. As he reflected on that care, he realized that it was very much like the care of a shepherd for his sheep (vv. 1-4) and the care of a host for his guests (vv. 5-6).

David was very familiar with both. Much of his time during his boyhood years was occupied with the care of his father's sheep, and one of his duties as a king was hosting guests.

In this psalm, the sandal is on the other foot. Here David is not the shepherd but the sheep and not the host but the guest, and it is none other than the Lord God himself who is doing the shepherding and the hosting.

How often we surf across the Scriptures without truly pondering what we are reading and without receiving the blessing such pondering brings! Think about the Lord caring for his people as a shepherd and host. What a privilege! And it is this sense of privilege that permeates and dominates this psalm. Peter Jeffery writes: 'Psalm 23 is pre-eminently a psalm of privilege. It speaks throughout of what God does for his people. ... David is not praying in this Psalm, he is not asking God to do something for him. Rather he is rejoicing in what the Lord has done and continues to do in his life.'[1]

Let's walk through Psalm 23 and breathe the fresh air of privilege that gently blows throughout.

Confidence in the Lord's shepherdly care (vv. 1-4)

David begins with this wonderful affirmation:

> The LORD is my shepherd;
> I shall not want.

How astonishing it is to find the words 'LORD' and 'shepherd' in such proximity! David is asserting that the Sovereign Ruler of the universe has taken up the menial task of shepherding him! We could not dare believe this if the Lord himself had not revealed himself in this way (Gen. 49:24).

Christians cannot read David's words without having their thoughts immediately rise to these words from the Lord Jesus Christ: 'I am the good shepherd. The good shepherd gives his life for the sheep' (John 10:11).

Through his redeeming death on the cross, Christ purchased his sheep. The wrath of God was, as it were, hurtling towards them, and Jesus stepped between them and the wrath and absorbed it on their behalf.

Having purchased his sheep on the cross, the Lord Jesus now lovingly tends them along the lines described in this psalm.

When believers read the opening words of Psalm 23, they cannot help but insert the name 'Jesus' between 'Lord' and 'is', saying, 'The Lord Jesus is my shepherd.' This is as natural for them as breathing.

Having affirmed that the Lord is his shepherd, David proceeds to describe the care he had received from the Lord. It was the best possible care from the best possible shepherd. There is more than one shepherd for us in this world. The devil himself is a shepherd who feeds on his own sheep (Ps. 49:14). But there is only one Lord—the Lord God. And this is the one whom David had as his shepherd. True religion resides in being able to say with David: 'The LORD is my shepherd.' It is a matter of that personal pronoun 'my'— saying to God 'my Lord' and having the assurance that he says in return 'my child'.

David celebrated the Lord's shepherdly care in both life (vv. 1-3) and death (v. 4).

The Lord's care in this life (vv. 1-3)

With the Lord as his shepherd, David knew no want or lack. His needs were met by his shepherd. Although he most certainly did not have everything he could desire, he had everything he needed. And God's people of every generation do not lack:

FOOD They do not lack food because they are made to lie down in green pastures.

This has to do with finding rest in the Word of God. The 'green pastures' represent food to the sheep. The lying down represents leisure or time. By the grace of the Lord, then, his people spend time meditating on the food which he has prepared for them, which is the Word of God.

We can go further and say that the Lord provides a green pasture for his sheep every time the Word of God is truly preached. This challenges all who know the Lord to prize biblical preaching heartily. And it soundly rebukes all those 'preachers' who lead their people away from the green grass the Lord has provided in his Word to the brown, withered grass of human wisdom.

All God's people have been given rest from the guilt of sin and the fear of condemnation through the redeeming work of Christ. They are God's people by virtue of that. But they still need rest from hunger, from annoying parasites and from conflict. We find these as we look to the green pastures in the Word of God. We are either grazing in those pastures or we are straying from our shepherd.

REFRESHMENT They do not lack refreshment because they are led beside still waters.

God's people often find themselves in need of spiritual refreshment. This is so because they walk in a wearying and exhausting world. Even their 'fellow-sheep' can be trying at times!

Where is the needed refreshment to be found? Are we not refreshed when we contemplate the greatness of our God? Do we not find it when we ponder his glorious plan of salvation in which he placed his love on us before time, appointed his Son to be our Redeemer, sent him in the fullness of time and accepted on our behalf his sinless life and atoning death? Are we not refreshed by pondering Christ's ongoing intercession for us? Are we not rejuvenated by calling to mind his promise to come again and receive us unto himself into eternal glory?

All of these refreshing things—and many, many more—are found in the Word of God. So we are back to the Bible again! It is green pasture in which we may feed and refreshing water from which we may drink.

FORGIVENESS AND RENEWAL They do not lack forgiveness and renewal because their souls are restored.

Sheep stray, and so do followers of the Lord Jesus. But his kind shepherdly care covers even that. A straying sheep is still a sheep, and the Lord ever cares for his own. David himself would stray far, but he did not—could not!—stray beyond the long reach of the arm of grace (2 Sam. 11:1-12:15; Ps. 32:1-11).

In the New Testament, we need look no further than Simon Peter to find an example of a straying saint who was pursued, forgiven and restored by his divine shepherd (John 18:15-18,25-27; 21:15-19).

Every child of God is in the grip of grace—mighty, unrelenting, stubborn, pursuing grace!

DIRECTION AND GUIDANCE They do not lack direction and guidance because they are led in paths of righteousness.

Christians often vex themselves with the question of whether they are 'finding the Lord's will' for their lives. What consolation we have in this part of the Lord's shepherdly care! The Lord has promised to lead his people. We should not concern ourselves so much, then, with finding the Lord's will as with walking close to the Lord. Peter Jeffery well says: 'Our problem is not really one of guidance, it is one of closeness to God.'[2]

It is important to notice that the Lord always leads his people in 'paths of righteousness', that is, in conformity with what God has revealed in his Word. This verse will not allow us to claim the Lord's leadership for any action that is opposed to the Word of God.

The fact that the Lord leads his people 'For his name's sake' means that he guides them according to all that his name represents. His guidance is, then, in keeping with his holiness, his love, his faithfulness, his wisdom and all that he has revealed himself to be.

The Lord's care in death (v. 4)

It is only natural for us to shrink from physical death, which is the separation of body and soul. Death is an intruder into God's creation. It came into this world as a result of mankind's sinful rebellion against God. But, as Matthew Henry notes, the terror of the word 'death' quickly gives way to 'four words which lessen the terror'.[3]

SHADOW A dark shadow may appear to be quite frightening but it has no real power to harm us. And death, unpleasant and forbidding as it may be, cannot finally do any real harm to the child of God. Henry T. Mahan writes: ' … Christ has removed the substance of death and only a shadow remains. A shadow is there but cannot hurt or destroy.'[4]

VALLEY While admitting that the valley is 'deep indeed, and dark, and dirty', Matthew Henry calls it a fruitful place and concludes that death offers 'fruitful comforts to God's people'.[5]

WALK David describes his activity in the valley as walking, which is regarded as pleasant and restful.

THROUGH How thankful we should be for this word! The valley of death is not the stopping place for the children of God. It is a travelling place. Matthew Henry notes that the saints of God will not get lost in it but will come out safely.[6]

The Lord himself was the basis of David's peace about

death. As David contemplates his death, he sees himself entering a dark valley. Suddenly he is aware that someone else is there in the shadows. It is the Lord himself. As he gazes upon his Lord, David sees that he is carrying a rod and staff. The rod was a heavy club the shepherd used to kill predators, and the staff, a long pole with a crook in one end, used to round up the sheep and to guide them along.

> It is only natural for us to shrink from physical death, which is the separation of body and soul. Death is an intruder into God's creation.

The sight of those instruments causes David to realize that he has absolutely nothing to fear. His shepherd is there to kill the enemies of fear, doubt and guilt and to guide him safely through. The same Lord who was shepherding him through life would shepherd him through death.

It is important to notice the change in personal pronoun as David reflects on his shepherd. In verses 2 and 3, David speaks about his shepherd (notice the fourfold use of 'he'). But when he comes to the valley of death, David drops the 'he' in favour of 'you' and 'your'. He was able to look upon the prospect of death with peace and tranquillity because he knew that it would mean meeting his glorious shepherd face to face.

If we would have the same peace about death as David, we must have the same shepherd. We must always keep in mind as we deal with this psalm that it is all predicated upon the opening line: 'The LORD is my shepherd'.

We cannot have what the shepherd produces without having the shepherd. If we want to enjoy the full measure of David's peace, we must have the full measure of his faith. We must recognize that we desperately need a shepherd. We must recognize that only God can rightly shepherd us. And we must wholeheartedly turn to God, renouncing our reliance on ourselves and on any other shepherds.

On the basis of what David says about death in this psalm, Matthew Henry writes: 'A child of God may meet the messengers of death and receive its summons with a holy security and serenity of mind.'7

Confidence in the Lord's care as a host (vv. 5-6)

John R. W. Stott writes: 'The scene changes. I am no longer out of doors, but indoors; no longer a sheep in a flock, but a guest at a banquet.' 8

We can go even further. God's children are his guests because they are his friends. They were not always so. They were by nature God's enemies. But he has reconciled them to himself through the cross of Christ (Eph. 2:14-18; Col. 1:19-22). Think of it! Friends of God! What a privilege!

As the shepherd cares for the needs of his sheep, so the host provides for the needs of his friends. David pictured the shepherd's care as beginning in this life and ending in death. With this picture of the host, he again starts with this life, but he carries it beyond death into the life to come.

God as host in this life (v. 5)

David affirms that God's provisions for his guests are both constant and abundant.

The constancy of God's provisions means that God's people have them in every situation and circumstance. We have already noted that the saints of God have enemies in the hour of death. They have them all through life as well. These enemies are the world, the flesh and the devil.

Knowing about these enemies, David here subjects God's care to what we might call the ultimate test. He asserts that God's care cannot be negated or destroyed by these fierce enemies. David sees himself sitting at a banquet table while they gather all around. While they threaten and snarl, he feasts. Such is the care of God!

David emphasizes the abundance of God's care in these terms:

You anoint my head with oil;

My cup runs over.

(v. 5b).

It was customary in those days to receive a guest by anointing him with fragrant perfume and with a cup filled with a choice wine. In this way, the host indicated that nothing was to be considered too good for his guest.

David declares that God's care surpasses even this. His head had been anointed, and his cup was overflowing.

Such care compelled David to say:

Surely goodness and mercy

shall follow me

All the days of my life; …

(v. 6a).

God's goodness is that disposition which causes him actively to seek the wellbeing of his creature. His mercy is that quality that inclines him to relieve misery. Because he había seen so very much of God's faithful care in every conceivable situation, David knew he could count on God's goodness and mercy every step of the way.

God as host in the life to come (v. 6b)

The provisions of God in this life are a small foretaste of what awaits believers. The table of which David has spoken is set in the midst of enemies in the wilderness. A glorious day is coming when all God's people will be gathered around God's table in his everlasting house, and there no enemy will be present to offer a single snarl.

So the greatest expression of the goodness and mercy of God awaits us in heaven. The people of God will then be with the Lord who cared for them every step of the way. And they will never be separated from him.

FOR FURTHER STUDY

1. Read John 10:11-18. What do these verses teach about the shepherdly care of the Lord Jesus?
2. Read John 11:25-26, 2 Corinthians 5:1-8 and 1 Thessalonians 4:13-18. What are some reasons Christians need not fear death?

TO THINK ABOUT AND DISCUSS

1. Discuss with some friends what Psalm 23 means to you. Ask them to do the same with you.
2. Write down some of the expressions of God's 'goodness and mercy' that you have experienced.

5 Pilgrimage psalms

A quick look

These psalms were sung by pilgrims travelling to Jerusalem for the annual feasts held there: 43; 46; 48; 84; 87; 120-134. The first of these feasts, the Passover, celebrated that night in Egypt when God's death angel passed over the firstborn of Israelites who were in houses marked by blood (Exod. 11:1-12:51) while the firstborn of the Egyptians were slain. That event led to Israel being delivered from their long bondage in Egypt.

The second of the annual festivals was 'The Feast of Weeks', also known as Pentecost. Celebrated seven weeks or fifty days after the Passover, it was essentially a harvest celebration (Exod. 34:22; Lev. 23:15-16; Deut. 16:9-10,16).

The 'Feast of Tabernacles', also called the 'Feast of Ingathering', lasted seven days. The people spent these days dwelling in temporary booths. This reminded them of their fathers who dwelt in such booths during the years of wilderness wandering. It also celebrated the settlement of their fathers in a land where they could plant crops and enjoy the fruit of the earth (Exod. 23:14-17; 34:22; Lev. 23:39-44; Deut. 16:13-17).

A closer look

Psalm 48

We cannot identify the author of this psalm. It is simply attributed to 'the sons of Korah'. It is the psalm about the magnificence of the city of Jerusalem.

We may well imagine this author being a citizen of Jerusalem for a long time, probably from birth. We picture him going through his childhood, teenage and early adult years without giving much thought to the city. One day, perhaps in his middle age, he takes a stroll around the city and realizes something of its splendour. He returns to his home and writes this psalm for his fellow-citizens, urging them to walk around Jerusalem to take note of her beauty as he had.

It is important for us to realize that there had been no change in the city at all. Its glory had been there all along. The change was rather in the psalmist himself.

The city of Jerusalem, often referred to as 'Zion', has been taken by generations of Christians to be a picture of the church and of the heavenly city to come. We might say it is a picture of both the church in this world and the church at rest.

Like Jerusalem of old, the church has a beauty about her. As Jerusalem was 'elevated' (v. 2) by virtue of the mountainous region in which she was located, the church enjoys spiritual elevation by virtue of having been visited and blessed by God.

The church is also glorious, as was Jerusalem of old, because the Lord himself has taken up residence in her (v. 3).

Furthermore, the church, like Jerusalem once again, has been given a marvellous defence (vv. 12-13). The Lord himself is her preserver and defender, even to the point that the gates of hell cannot possibly triumph over her (Matt. 16:18).

Psalms 120-134

These psalms are identified as 'Songs of Ascents' because they were sung by pilgrims making their way to Jerusalem which was, as noted above, located in a mountainous area (Ps. 48:1-2; 125:1-2). These pilgrims had to 'ascend' to get there.

It is possible that these songs were so named for another reason, namely, what the pilgrims themselves experienced as they journeyed. As they ascended to Jerusalem to attend its annual festivals, their hearts ascended within them. If this was indeed the case, these hymns speak very pointedly to us about how we regard public worship. Can we say that our hearts ascend within us as we anticipate worship in the house of God? We should regard worship in the Lord's house with the Lord's people as the highlight of the week and look forward to it more and more with each passing day.

Psalm 133

One of the Songs of Ascents, this psalm beautifully strikes the note of unity among the people of God. Firstly, David affirms the beauty of unity (v. 1). He declares it to be both good and pleasant. It is good in that it is pleasing to God, and it is pleasant in that it brings delight and happiness to those who experience it.

Secondly, David illustrates the beauty of unity (v. 2) by

referring to the anointing of Aaron and the dew of Mount Hermon (vv. 2-3).

Why did David choose the anointing of Aaron to illustrate unity? Perhaps the reason is that Aaron's high priestly work was a unifying factor for the nation. Once each year, he went into the Most Holy Place of the tabernacle with the blood of a sacrifice to offer an atonement for the sins of the people. Israel was not just a political entity. It was a spiritual entity in which the people were unified by a blood atonement.

> Unity among the people of God is always fragrant and makes them appealing to unbelievers. But the odour of disunity will drive them away!

Christians today have the very same basis for unity. Like the people of faith in Israel of old, we have been called into a covenant relationship with God and one another on the basis of the atonement of the Lord Jesus Christ.

The oil Moses used to anoint Aaron was made especially for that purpose and in accordance with God's specifications. This oil was to be poured profusely upon Aaron, even to the point that it dripped from his beard and fell on the border or collar of his robe. So much oil was used that all those who were witnessing the event could easily smell its sweet fragrance.

Unity among the people of God is always fragrant and makes them appealing to unbelievers. But the odour of disunity will drive them away!

David also illustrated unity by mentioning Mount

Hermon. The highest mountain in Syria, it could be seen 120 miles away. It was also known for its moisture. For two-thirds of the year, it is covered with snow, and it receives sixty inches of precipitation annually. It is the main source of supply for the Jordan River.

Perhaps David could see this mountain as he wrote this psalm. He thought about how refreshing was its dew. Unity is also refreshing. Discord tires, but unity reinvigorates.

The moisture of Mount Hermon also ensured productivity. It flowed down to the plains to water the crops. And unity is productive in the church as well. A divided church is always a distracted church. The dissension becomes the focal point. But unity allows the church to focus on its high task and glorious privilege of preaching the gospel.

FOR FURTHER STUDY

1. Read Matthew 16:13-20. What does Jesus teach here about the church?
2. Read Ephesians 5:22-33. What does the apostle Paul teach in these verses about the church?

TO THINK ABOUT AND DISCUSS

1. What are some things about your church that cause you to rejoice?
2. The 'Songs of Ascents' are songs of those preparing to worship. Write down some practical ways in which you can prepare for public worship.

6 An even closer look: Psalm 84

ublic worship is part of God's design for his people. He doesn't suggest it or request it. He commands it. If we truly feel gratitude for our redemption, we will not only obey this command but will also do so with the intense desire expressed by this psalmist. And when we intensely desire worship, we will inevitably find ourselves immensely enjoying the blessings that flow from it.

This psalmist, who is left unidentified, takes us to one of the most prominent features of Jewish life—that is, a pilgrimage to the temple in Jerusalem. That temple was, of course, the centre of Jewish life. While the Jews understood that their God was so great that 'even the highest heaven' could not 'contain' him (1 Kings 8:27, NIV), they also realized that he had been pleased, in a sense, to make the temple his dwelling-place.

This psalmist relates something of how he felt about travelling with others to the temple for religious festivals held there each year. We need to let the delight he felt about public worship at the temple speak to us about our attitude towards public worship today.

Intense longing for worship (vv. 1-4)

In the first place, we must note his intense longing for worship (vv. 1-4). How great was this longing? The psalmist says it consumed his entire being. He says his soul 'faints' with this longing (v. 2). It was almost too much for him to bear.

As he thought about the house of the Lord and its worship, he found himself envying the birds that nested there (v. 3). He may have also referred to these birds to convey something of the benefits of worship. The sparrow is a common emblem for worthlessness (Matt. 10:29-31) and the swallow a common symbol for restlessness. The house of God ministers to both!

The psalmist also expressed envy of those who were always at the temple—that is, the priests.

We must make sure we do not miss the reason for such intense longing. It was because the public worship in the temple was the worship of the LORD of hosts (v. 1). The 'hosts' are the heavenly hosts or the heavenly powers. The Lord God is the creator of all the heavenly beings and is their ruler. As such he is worthy of our worship.

We will never feel like worshipping God until we understand something of his greatness, and we cannot help but worship once we do. In other words, there is a direct correlation between our conception of God and our desire for worship. The greater God is in our eyes, the greater will be our desire to worship him.

What can we say of ourselves on this matter of desiring public worship? The sad fact is many who profess to know the Lord have very little or no appetite at all for worship.

It is obvious that many don't have anything near the intensity of desire this psalmist expresses. What they lack in desire they make up for in excuses, and many of these are so absurd as to be almost unbelievable.

One of my fellow-pastors had a church member who refused to attend church because he claimed to be unable to sit on a pew for any length of time. But one day this pastor passed by the pool hall and noticed this gentleman sitting there. Three hours later the pastor went by the pool hall again and noticed the man sitting in the same place. The pastor, thinking the pool hall must have had some very comfortable seats, went inside. The only seats he found were old, unpadded church pews!

The immense blessings of worship (vv. 5-7)

In addition to describing the intensity of his longing for worship, this psalmist proceeds to share the immense blessings that flow from worship.

In these verses the psalmist looks around at his fellow-pilgrims. He sees in them the same intensity of desire that he himself knew, and he calls them 'blessed' or 'happy'.

The psalmist's point is clear. The pilgrims who had a flaming desire for worship were happy indeed.

What is there about worship that causes a person to be blessed? Some of the things the psalmist stresses are:

Strength

We would expect to read that with each passing day the pilgrims grew more and more weary until finally their strength was depleted.

'Not so,' says the psalmist. In fact, just the opposite was the case. The closer the pilgrims got to the city of Jerusalem, the stronger they became. Their love for worship was so great that the mere anticipation of it had an energizing effect upon them.

The strength they received from anticipating worship was so great that even the Valley of Baca did not bother them (v. 6). This was a particularly arid and barren valley that pilgrims had to traverse on their way to Jerusalem. It was undoubtedly the most arduous and difficult part of the journey. But they were so lost in their anticipation of worship that this valley seemed like an oasis to them.

How we need to let this picture sink into our hearts! We do not have to make long pilgrimages through treacherous terrain to reach the house of God. But it is not too far-fetched to suggest that each week is something like a pilgrimage back to the house of God for his people. During that pilgrimage, we often find ourselves in the Valley of Baca. But, happily, those who are faithful to worship God find that they have strength for traversing that valley. Drawing strength from the previous Sunday's worship and anticipating the next Sunday's worship, they go from 'strength to strength' (v. 7). They have, therefore, the strength that is needed to face life's trials and hardships.

Satisfaction

The psalmist also emphasizes the satisfaction that public worship provides. In the last part of his psalm, he prays to the Lord (vv. 8-12). In the course of this prayer, he says:

For a day in your courts is
better than a thousand.
I would rather be a doorkeeper
in the house of my God

than dwell in the tents of
wickedness
(v. 10).

What a contrast there is here! On the one hand, there is a
very limited period of time, a day, and a very limited contact,
a doorkeeper, that is, one who only stood at the entrance. On
the other hand, the psalmist pictures one who dwells in the
tents of wickedness. Here we have
a prolonged period of time and
intimate contact. This wicked
man does not spend just a day in
wickedness, and he does not just
stand at the door of it. He goes
into it and sits there in ease.

> The slightest contact with God through real, heartfelt worship is more satisfying than the deepest involvement in sin.

Do we understand what the
psalmist is saying? The slightest
contact with God through real,
heartfelt worship is more
satisfying than the deepest involvement in sin. The sinful life
is always promising satisfaction, and the deeper one goes into
it, the less satisfaction he finds. But the deeper one goes into
public worship, the more satisfaction he finds.

What makes worship so satisfying to us? It brings us into
contact with the eternal God who delights in being a sun and
a shield to those who love him and serve him (v. 11). As we
worship him, he gives us grace and glory and every 'good
thing' (v. 11).

Nothing can be more satisfying than having the light of
God shining on our pathway and having the shield of God to
protect us from evil. Nothing is more satisfying than

receiving grace for living and glory for the future. Nothing is more satisfying than knowing God will not withhold from those who truly worship him anything they need.

The life of sin offers us no light, no shield, no grace, and no glory. It offers only darkness, danger, grief, and ruin. And—solemn thought!—when the people of God do not delight themselves in the worship of almighty God, they make their company with those who dwell in the tents of wickedness and rob themselves of immense satisfaction. No, children of God do not lose their salvation when they fail to worship God, but they certainly act as if they have more in common with the wicked than they do with the people of God.

FOR FURTHER STUDY

1. Psalm 84:3 mentions sparrows and swallows. Read Matthew 6:25-26. What point does Jesus make from 'the birds of the air'?
2. Read Isaiah 40:27-31. What do these verses teach about receiving strength from God?

TO THINK ABOUT AND DISCUSS

1. Jot down some of the blessings which you receive in public worship. How do these things strengthen you?
2. Make a list of some friends to invite to public worship.

7 Individual laments

A quick look

The psalms of lament consist of urgent and fervent cries to God from stressful and troubling circumstances. These psalms can be divided into individual and communal laments. The former may deal with such things as sickness, the betrayal of a friend or, as we shall soon see, the keen consciousness of having sinned against God.

Some examples of individual laments are: 3-7; 12; 13; 22; 25-28; 35; 38-40; 42-44; 51; 54-57; 77.

A closer look

Psalm 3

This psalm is one of the fourteen that are linked with actual events from David's life (7; 18; 30; 34; 51; 52; 54; 56; 57; 59; 60; 63; 142).

This psalm consists of David's lament when his son, Absalom, attempted to overthrow him. While his troubles were monumental, David found peace and strength in the Lord. Steven J. Lawson says of this psalm: 'It is a hymn of individual lament, written to paint a clear picture of what triumphant faith looks like when it is tested by the fires of adversity.'[1]

This is the first psalm in which we find the word 'Selah'. This term comes to us from the world of music. When a composer put 'Selah' into his music, he was calling for a rest, a pause or a hush. Every musician knows the importance of this. A conductor stands before an orchestra or choir with a baton in his hand. With that baton he can call from that orchestra or choir a thunderous burst or dead silence. When he calls for the latter, the whole composition takes on special meaning.

The placement of the three 'Selahs' in this psalm leads us to draw three conclusions.

THE SELAH OF TROUBLE

Firstly, we should learn to view the troubles of life as 'Selah' times (vv. 1-2). The first 'Selah' that David penned was not one he would have chosen. It was forced upon him. He was facing the greatest trial of his life. His son had rebelled and their respective armies were about to join in battle.

There is more. Absalom had evidently made it his business to ridicule David's faith. He and his supporters were saying:

'There is no help for him in

God'

(v. 2).

David's troubles lead us to think about our own. We also have circumstances which cause us to pause and reflect. Sickness is such a time. So is the death of a loved one. And so are those times in which our faith, like David's of old, is being challenged.

THE SELAH OF FAITH

Secondly, we should always move from the 'Selah' of trouble to the 'Selah' of faith (vv. 3-4).

David did not allow the challenge to his faith to cause him to abandon it. He met the challenge to his faith by confessing his faith. He specifically confessed his faith in God as a shield which would protect him. This was not wishful thinking on David's part. God had protected him many times!

He also calls God 'his glory' (v. 3), or the one in whom he gloried. This is surely a confession of the majesty and sovereignty of God. Our trials become less trying when we place them in the glare of the greatness of God.

Further, he confesses his faith in the tender compassion of God for him. He, the Lord, is the one who lifts the head (v. 3). When David's head fell to his chest in dejection and despondency, the Lord was there to encourage him.

Finally, he confesses his faith in the readiness of God to answer prayer (v. 4). Charles Spurgeon writes: 'We need not fear a frowning world while we rejoice in a prayer-hearing God.'[2]

THE SELAH OF PEACE AND JOY

The third and final 'Selah' leads us to this conclusion: The 'Selah' of faith will invariably lead us to the 'Selah' of peace and joy. Having reminded himself of his God in verses 3 and 4, David is able to write:

I lay down and slept;
I awoke, for the LORD
sustained me.

I will not be afraid of ten
thousands of people
Who have set themselves
against me all around
(vv. 5-6).

Psalm 77

The first thing that we note about this psalm is that its author, Asaph, was a very unhappy man. In verse 2, he mentions the day of his trouble. In the same verse, he tells us that this trouble was so deep and serious that his soul refused to be comforted. In verse 3 he affirms that even the thought of God did not comfort him. He also describes himself as being 'overwhelmed' in that same verse.

Verse 4 adds even more dark strokes to his description. His trouble was such that he could find no respite in sleep, and he found himself to be incapable of even talking about it. Most of us find relief from sharing our troubles with others, but Asaph could not even do this.

Why was he so deeply disturbed? It all came about from his considering the past (v. 5). And what was there about the past that caused him to be so despondent? Was there some glaring failure there? Surprisingly enough, the past was good. It was a time in which he had enjoyed 'a song in the night' (v. 6).

This is puzzling. Why would a good past cause Asaph to be so exercised? And the answer is that it made him sharply conscious of how his present circumstances did not measure up. He could look at the past and see marvellous instances of God at work in his life and in the lives of those around him. But the present seemed to be utterly devoid of such instances.

It was of such a nature that it appeared as if God had cast him off for ever (v. 7), had decided to be favourable no more (v. 7), had caused his mercy to cease for ever (v. 8), had failed to keep what he had promised (v. 8), had forgotten to be gracious (v. 9) and had, in anger, locked up all his tender mercies and thrown away the key (v. 9).

The good news is that Asaph did not continue in his distress. In verse 10 he turns the corner and begins to come out of his misery and woe. As he reflected on the past, he began to realize that he had been looking at it in the wrong way. Instead of letting past glory depress him, he should have been letting it bless him. The fact that God had worked mightily in the past meant there was hope for the future. The God of the past had not changed! He is the same God. No matter how great the darkness of present circumstances, it is not greater than God.

There are two phrases in this psalm that never fail to catch my eye. One is in verse 13 and the other in verse 19. In the former, we are told that God's way is in the sanctuary. In the latter, we are told that his way is in the sea. We have a tendency to want to track God through the sea. We want to know why he does this and why he doesn't do that. We should rather focus on seeking him in the sanctuary. In public worship, we can so meet God that we become satisfied with the fact that he is God. When we are satisfied with God as he is, we will find ourselves no longer troubled by what he does.

FOR FURTHER STUDY

1. Read 2 Samuel 15:1-11,30. How did Absalom become so strong? How did David and those loyal to him leave Jerusalem?
2. Read Joshua 24:1-15. How did Joshua use Israel's past in this passage?

TO THINK ABOUT AND DISCUSS

1. David spoke of his increased troubles (Ps. 3:1). Write down some things that are troubling you. What should you do about these things?
2. What can you do to help yourself when you feel as Asaph expressed in Psalm 77:7-9?

8 An even closer look: Psalm 51

This is one of the seven 'penitential' psalms (see also 6, 32, 40, 102, 130, 143). It is David's prayer of repentance after Nathan the prophet had confronted him with his sins (2 Sam. 12). David had committed adultery with Bathsheba and had covered it up by having her husband killed and taking her as his wife (thereby making it appear as if the child was the premature by-product of their marriage).

David responded to Nathan's message by saying, 'I have sinned' (2 Sam. 12:13), and then, we may suppose, slipped away to a quiet place to pray along the lines recorded here.

As we analyse this psalm, we can discern three distinct elements.

David admits his sin (vv. 1-5)

The seriousness of it (vv. 1-3)

The fact that David uses four words to describe his sin shows that he is not trying to evade the issue or trivialize it. 'Transgressions' refer to rebellion or deliberately crossing over a boundary. 'Iniquity' suggests a perverseness or twistedness. 'Sin' is falling short of God's standard or missing the target God has set. 'Evil' (v. 4) simply refers to the ugly, repulsive nature of sin against God.

The essence of it (v. 4)

Here David comes to grips with the issue that makes sin such a serious matter. It is the creature thumbing his nose at his Creator. Sin is directed against God. It is nothing less than saying we wish God were not God and that his laws would disappear.

It is true that David also sinned against Bathsheba, Uriah, and even the whole nation of Israel, but it is God who defines proper behaviour towards others. Any sin against others is ultimately, then, a sin against the God who set these boundaries.

The origin of it (v. 5)

David leaves no stone unturned in his repentance. Here he goes to the very root of sin—human nature. We sin because we are born sinners. In doing this, David is not seeking to excuse himself but is rather taking an honest, hard look at the truth about himself.

David honours God (vv. 4b-6)

By accepting the rightness of God's verdict (v. 4b)

In acknowledging his sin, David was agreeing with God about it. Prior to his confession, he was in a state of disputing with God. God was, as it were, on one side of the fence, and he, David, on the other. Here, however, he leaps over the fence and joins God in condemning his sin.

By acknowledging the correctness of God's standard (v. 6)

David further recognizes that God's standard for behaviour is right, and that standard is not only outward conformity to God's laws, but inward delight in them.

David pleads for mercy (vv. 1-2,7-12)

The basis of this plea (v. 1)

Some might think David to be terribly audacious. How could he possibly muster the courage to ask for mercy from the very one he had so deeply offended? The answer is he knew something of the nature of God, that he is lovingly kind and delights in showing 'tender mercies'.

The nature of this plea (vv. 1-2,7-12)

David wasn't content just to mutter a quick 'forgive me for all my sins.' His repentance was thorough and earnest. He sees his sins being written in a book, and he longs for God to blot out that handwriting (vv. 1,9). He sees them as being a deep stain and longs to be thoroughly washed and cleansed by God (vv. 2,7—'hyssop', used by priests in cleansing rituals, symbolizes cleansing). He sees his sins as being robbers of his joy and gladness, and desires the restoration of these things (vv. 8,12).

He further sees his sins as the cause of God's chastisement (v. 8—'the bones you have broken'), and he desires to have that chastisement lifted. He sees his sins as provoking God to avert his face, and now he longs to have God's face turned towards him again (v. 9). He sees his heart being polluted by his sins and desires to have a clean heart (v. 10).

He sees his sins depriving him of his steadfastness in the Lord's ways, and longs to have that changed (v. 10). He sees his sins depriving him of God's presence and God's spirit, and longs for these to be reversed (v. 11). He sees his sins trampling him and prays to be upheld (v. 12).

These things lead to two conclusions: (1) David took sin with utmost seriousness (2) David believed in a God who abounds in mercy.

The confidence of this plea (vv. 13,17)

A twofold confidence gripped David's heart as he offered this prayer to God. Firstly, he knew that God could use his experience to influence others (v. 13). Secondly, he knew that God would not fail to hear his plea (v. 17). Psalm 32, the sequel to this psalm, shows that God did indeed hear David's prayer.

FOR FURTHER STUDY

1. Read 2 Samuel 11. Write down each sin that David committed in this chapter.
2. Use a concordance to find other occasions when someone said, 'I have sinned.'

TO THINK ABOUT AND DISCUSS

1. How do you feel when you know that you have done something to disobey God?
2. Using David's prayer as a model, write your own prayer for forgiveness.

9 Communal laments

A quick look

The common theme running through these psalms is concern for the spiritual state of the nation of Israel. The primary application of these psalms is not to any single nation today, but rather to the church.

Some examples of communal laments are to be seen in the following psalms: 59-61; 63; 64; 69-71; 74; 79; 80; 83; 85; 86; 88; 90; 126.

A closer look

Psalm 60

It was during a time of sparkling success that David wrote this psalm. The heading indicates that it was written in conjunction with David's resounding victory over the Syrians in the Valley of Salt (2 Sam. 8:13).

This psalm enables us to peer into what went into that victory. It relates a prayer that David offered to God as he and his forces were engaged in conflict with the Syrians. It falls into three major parts. Verses 1-3 consist of David's sad lament before God. Verses 4-8 reflect his solemn pleading with God. The final section, composed of verses 9-12, presents David's confident rejoicing before the Lord.

These three emphases merge to make it clear that any success enjoyed by the children of God must ultimately be traced to their gracious Lord who is constantly at work in the lives of his children.

DAVID'S SAD LAMENT BEFORE GOD (VV. 1-3)

The opening words of David's psalm cast a far different light on David's victory over the Syrians. It was not an easy triumph at all. It evidently came only after an initial defeat at the hands of the Syrians.

David did not attribute this defeat to 'bad luck' or poor military strategy. He and the people of Israel were in a covenant relationship with God. One aspect of this relationship was God's promises to give them victory over their enemies if they, the people of God, would walk in obedience to his commandments (Deut. 28:1,7).

Defeat at the hands of an enemy had, therefore, to be understood and interpreted in terms of the spiritual condition of the people.

Perhaps the string of successes under David's leadership had created a false sense of security that caused the people to take for granted the blessing of God apart from their obedience.

This much was clear to David: God had allowed his people to suffer a humiliating defeat because he was sorely displeased with them (v. 1). This defeat was of such a staggering nature that it seemed to David as if God had made the earth itself to tremble (v. 2). It was so overwhelming that it had left the people of God as disoriented as a man that was reeling under the influence of wine (v. 3).

All of this made it most urgent for David and his people to seek the Lord earnestly, and in the remaining verses of the psalm we find David, as the head of the nation, doing exactly that. It is very likely that he also led the nation to join him in his heartfelt seeking of God.

David's personal pleading with God is composed of three strands of argument.

The Lord's banner (v. 4)

Firstly, David holds the thought of a banner before the Lord. God had special purposes in making the people of Israel his special possession. One of these was that the nation might be a banner to surrounding nations. In other words, Israel was to be a banner that proclaimed God's truth. Others were to be able to look at her and see the truth about God's redemption. Israel was to be like a placard before them, showing the reality of that redemption and the difference it had made in their lives.

When the people of God suffered defeat at the hand of their enemies, her enemies would be inclined to conclude that there was nothing to the faith of Israel. Israel's defeat would, as it were, cause the banner of truth to be dragged along behind her rather than fly victoriously over her. David's prayer was, therefore, that the Lord would now grant victory to his people so the banner he had given them would again fly high and the truth would be known.

Moses employed the same argument with the Lord. When the people of Israel refused to enter the land of Canaan, the

Lord said to Moses, 'How long will these people reject me? And how long will they not believe me, with all the signs which I have performed among them? I will strike them with the pestilence and disinherit them, and I will make of you a nation greater and mightier than they' (Num. 14:11-12).

Moses responded to these words by saying, 'Now if you kill these people as one man, then the nations which have heard of your fame will speak, saying: "Because the LORD was not able to bring this people to the land which he swore to give them, therefore he killed them in the wilderness"' (Num. 14:15-16).

Having made that point, Moses proceeded to remind the Lord of his promise to pardon the sin of his people (Num. 14:17-19). Their sin had made their banner trail, but pardon would lift it again.

The Lord's beloved (v. 5)

David further appealed to the Lord by reminding him that he, David, had been chosen by the Lord as the king of the nation. David realized that this was all due to the Lord having placed his love upon him. David recognized that he, the beloved of the Lord, had been placed over a nation beloved by the Lord. As the head of that nation, he pleaded with the Lord to deliver him and the nation from the hardship that had come upon them.

Charles Spurgeon says of this portion of the psalm: 'Here is one suppliant for many, even as in the case of our Lord's intercession for his saints. He, the Lord's David, pleads for the rest of the beloved, beloved and accepted in him the Chief Beloved; he seeks salvation as though it were for himself, but his eye is ever upon all those who are one with him in the Father's love.'[2]

As the nation of Israel was blessed in and through David as her head, so the blessings of God flow to the church only through that beloved foreshadowed by David, the Lord Jesus Christ himself.

The Lord's promises (vv. 6-8)

David adds yet another dimension to his pleading for God's restored favour, that is, the promises of God. The enemies over whom he sought victory (v. 6) were those of whom the Lord had spoken (Gen. 15:18-21; Exod. 23:31; Num. 34:1-12).

David knew the promises of God were sure, and he prayed for victory on the basis of those promises. We would do well to emulate his example. Some turn faith into positive thinking that obligates God to do things he has not promised. But faith is not believing anything we want to believe. It is believing that God will do what he has promised and praying on the basis of those promises.

It may seem foolish to pray for something that God has already promised to do, but God is delighted when we parade his promises before him, and praying on the basis of those promises gives us assurance that our prayers will be heard and answered in the time and ways pleasing to God.

Spurgeon says of the assurance that comes from resting on the promises of God: 'Faith regards the promise not as fiction but fact, and therefore drinks in joy from it and grasps victory by it. "God hath spoken; I will rejoice;" here is a fit motto for every soldier of the cross.'[3]

That brings us to the final part of David's prayer —

DAVID'S CONFIDENT REJOICING BEFORE THE LORD (VV. 9-12)

David began his prayer in something of a turmoil, but now the storm has subsided and all is peaceful and calm. David knew the Lord would again lift his banner of truth, that he would deliver his beloved and keep his promises. There was, then, nothing to fear. The God who had momentarily 'cast off' his people in displeasure and had not gone out with their armies (v. 10) would, in light of the repentance of his people, give them help (v. 11).

Because God is faithful to return to his repentant people, David closes his psalm on this note of triumph:

Through God we will do

valiantly,

for it is he who shall tread

down our enemies

(v. 12).

David and the armies of Israel, as the eighth chapter of Second Samuel indicates, did indeed do valiantly. The initial defeat David described in the opening verses of Psalm 60 gave way to victory. David's dedicating of the spoils of war to the Lord (2 Sam. 8:11) shows that David knew his successes were not due to his skill and expertise but to the Lord. The author of Second Samuel makes this plain by twice saying 'the Lord preserved David wherever he went' (vv. 6,14). Furthermore, as Psalm 60 so abundantly proves, David understood that success from the Lord's hand comes as his people walk in a manner pleasing to him.

Psalm 63

David wrote this psalm while in the wilderness. The wilderness was a barren, desolate place where he was deprived of the comforts of home and exposed to bad weather and hostile enemies. 4

These things were in and of themselves enough to make the wilderness a very troubling and trying experience. David found it to be even more so for another reason. While in the wilderness he was away from the sanctuary of the Lord (v. 2).

There are those who tell us that the child of God should never go through a spiritual wilderness, that he should never feel barren and desolate spiritually. But most of us know that it is inevitable for us to have such times. Even though David was one of God's most favoured and blessed, he was not exempt from the wilderness experience he describes in this psalm.

The question is not whether we, as God's people, will have to go through wilderness experiences, but rather how to face them. It is at this point that David's psalm offers tremendous help.

OCCUPIED WITH GOD

It first shows us that David occupied himself with God and not with the wilderness.

How easy it would have been for David to occupy himself with his wilderness experience! The heading of this psalm tells us that it was written when David was in the wilderness of Judah. Why was he there? King Saul was seeking his life! (1 Sam. 22).

What a difficult time this was for David! Although the

prophet Samuel had anointed him to be Saul's successor, he appeared to be nowhere near coming to the throne. And although, he, David, had been nothing to the king except a loyal and devoted subject, he was a fugitive. He had gone into battle on behalf of Saul and Israel and defeated the giant Goliath. He had played soothing music to ease the anguish of the troubled and tormented Saul. But Saul, feeling no gratitude for these things, was filled with bitter envy and murderous rage towards David.

David certainly had moments when he allowed the difficulty of his situation to occupy him (1 Sam. 27:1), but this was the exception rather than the rule. For the most part, he responded to his difficulties and burdens by occupying himself with God.

This psalm is an example of this. David could have asked why these things were happening to him. He could have allowed himself to become bitter towards God. He could have begun to doubt whether the promises of God would be fulfilled.

Instead he begins this psalm by crying out:

O God, you are my God;

Early will I seek you;

My soul thirsts for you;

My flesh longs for you

In a dry and thirsty land

God's gracious covenant

It is not enough for us merely to observe that David occupied himself with God. He reminded himself of some particulars about God, namely, that he, God, had in grace entered into a covenant relationship with his people. It was on this basis and this basis alone that David was able to call him 'my God'.

God's lovingkindness
David also reminded himself of the lovingkindness of God, that is, those kind acts of God which flowed from a heart of love (v. 3). He further reminded himself of how God had been his help in the past (v. 7).

On the basis of God's kindness to him in the past, David knew he had nothing to fear. The same God who had tenderly cared for him could be counted on to continue to do the same.

With this psalm David teaches us one of the most important and vital lessons we can ever learn: the more occupied we are with God and his heart of love for his children, the more bearable our trials and difficulties will be.

RESOLVED TO PURSUE GOD

This psalm also shows us that David coped with his wilderness experience by resolving to pursue God vigorously.

This is a psalm of solemn resolve. David resolved to seek the Lord (v. 1), to bless the Lord (v. 4), and to lift up his hands, which was synonymous with prayer (v. 4, see also Ps. 38:2).

David was also determined to praise the Lord with 'joyful lips' (v. 5), to meditate on the Lord during the night (v. 6) and to rejoice in the Lord's protective care of him (v. 7).

All of this takes us a step further and shows us how to go about this business of occupying ourselves with God. It requires diligent and determined effort.

This brings us face to face with a gigantic failure in the

lives of many Christians—that is, desiring God's presence and his help in times of trial and difficulty without ever giving ourselves to a determined and devoted pursuit of God. We often want what God can give us rather than God himself.

PERSUADED OF GLORY IN THE FUTURE

Finally, this psalm shows us that David was able to cope with his wilderness because of his persuasion that he could see the glory and power of God even in the wilderness. David writes:

> So I have looked for you
> in the sanctuary,
> To see your power and
> your glory
> (v. 2).

Some take those words to mean that David was expressing his fervent hope that he would soon be delivered from his wilderness experience and once again be able to join in public worship. There can be no doubt that this was indeed the desire of David's heart.

But other scholars suggest that David was saying something quite different. They understand David to be addressing God in this way: 'I desire to see your glory and your power in the wilderness as I have seen it in the sanctuary'.

If this view is correct, David was reminding himself that God was not limited to the tabernacle. He certainly felt anguish over being separated from public worship, even as every child of God should feel a keen sense of loss when he is not able to be in the house of the Lord. But David knew the Lord could reveal himself right there in the wilderness. How wilderness living is transformed when one is able to see the glory and power of the Lord!

Perhaps the greatest question facing Christians today is this: do we believe we can see the glory and power of the Lord in the wilderness? Do we, as individuals, believe that the Lord can come to us in the midst of our difficulties and make his presence known to us? Do we believe the Lord can come to his entire church and bring renewal and power? Do we believe in revival for the church? Revival is that time when God comes to his church in the midst of the wilderness and pours out his blessings upon her, times in which he reveals his glory and power to her.

FOR FURTHER STUDY

1. Read 2 Samuel 8:1-18. Jot down some of the major successes of King David.
2. Read 1 Samuel 22:1-5. Where was David before he went into the wilderness of Judah? What happened while he was there?

TO THINK ABOUT AND DISCUSS

1. In Psalm 60:4, David mentions a 'banner of truth'. What does this imagery suggest to you?
2. What do you think it means to thirst and long for God?

10 An even closer look: Psalm 126

This psalm falls quite naturally into three parts. In verses 1-3, the psalmist speaks to his fellow-worshippers. In verse 4 he speaks to God. In verses 5-6, the Lord answers the psalmist.

The psalmist speaks to his fellow-worshippers (vv. 1-3)

The words of the psalmist to his fellow-worshippers deal with a remarkable episode in their history. The psalmist characterizes this time in this way:

When the LORD brought back
the captivity of Zion
(v. 1).

Most of the psalms were written during the reign of King David, but these words appear to take us to something that occurred many centuries after David, namely, the release of the Jews from captivity in Babylon.

The fact that most of the psalms were written during David's reign does not preclude later songs being added to the collection, and that is probably what happened in this instance.

We may rest assured that the Jews underwent a great spiritual renewal while they were in Babylon. While there, they came to see that their captivity was due to their sins, and they undoubtedly did a thorough job of repenting.

Then came the good news that they were going to be allowed to return to their homeland. The psalmist describes the torrent of joy that broke out when they received that word. He and his fellow-captives were 'like those who dream' (v. 1). The news was simply too good to be true!

He proceeds to describe the people laughing and singing (v. 2). Their joy was so great that other nations took note of it and concluded:

'The Lord has done great
things for them'
(v. 2).

There was no doubt in the psalmist's mind that it was indeed the Lord's doing. He begins the psalm by giving credit to the Lord (v. 1), and he wraps up this section by agreeing with what the other nations were saying: He essentially says, 'Yes, you are correct. The Lord has done great things for us.' Then he adds:

And we are glad
(v. 3).

The psalmist's description of this release from captivity is a wonderful and graphic description of every episode in which God has stepped into the lives of his people to grant them revival or spiritual renewal.

Revival always exceeds our expectations. Revival always opens the floodgates of joy. Revival always leaves a profound impression on those around the people of God.

The psalmist speaks to God (v. 4)

But from this joyous note, the psalmist moves to a sombre note. His re-living of the glory of their release from captivity suddenly causes him to realize that some slippage has taken place.

In other words, the people were not now as close to God as they had been when they were released from captivity. No, they hadn't gone back to the worship of idols (the captivity broke them of that once and for all), but they had somehow or other become complacent about the things of the Lord.

To get a true reading of what happened with these people after they returned to their land, one only has to read the prophecies of Malachi and Haggai. Malachi, for instance, talks about the people keeping up the round of religious activities without any sense of enthusiasm (Mal. 1:13). And Haggai talks about the people getting so occupied with their own business that they had little interest in the house of the Lord (Hag. 1:4).

We don't know just where the writer of Psalm 126 fits into the sequence of events that followed the release from captivity, but he had evidently seen enough to know that the euphoria of the release had faded and spiritual deterioration had set in.

So we find him praying in verse 4:

Bring back our captivity, O

Lord, as the streams in the South.

In other words, he was asking God to do for him and his

> Revival always exceeds our expectations. Revival always opens the floodgates of joy. Revival always leaves a profound impression on those around the people of God.

people something akin to what he had done when they were released from captivity. He is saying, 'Turn us back, O LORD, to that time.'

Their spiritual condition, at that time, reminded him of the southern region of their land. Drought always dried up the streams in that area, but then the rains would come and those dry stream beds would be filled with torrents of water.

With that picture in his mind, the psalmist was, therefore, asking God to do in the spiritual realm what he did in the natural realm. He was asking for a copious outpouring of God's power and grace, one that would take away their dryness and cause them to rejoice again.

The Lord speaks to the psalmist (vv. 5-6)

The Lord essentially says: 'Do you want what you had when you were released from captivity? Do you want a spiritual flood to relieve your dryness and barrenness? Then here is what you must do—you must sow in tears. If you will sow in tears, I promise that you will reap in joy.'

What was the Lord saying to this psalmist? He was calling upon him and all his people truly to repent of their sins, and then the flood of blessing would come.

We have noted that the people of God repented during their years of captivity in Babylon, and that repentance was as inextricably connected to their release and to the joy that sprang from it as the sowing of a farmer is connected to his reaping.

Now if they wanted to reap that same crop of joy and vibrancy, they would have to sow the same seeds. And if they were unwilling to sow those same seeds, they would have nothing to look forward to except continued spiritual dryness and lethargy.

These words ought to make certain truths very clear and obvious to us.

Firstly, if we want an explanation for spiritual decline, we have to look no further than the sins we have allowed to invade our lives.

Another truth that gleams at us from these verses is that sin is a very serious thing, and it has to be treated as such. If we want to reap the crop of spiritual renewal and vitality, we must sow 'in tears'.

A casual study of the great revivals of the past will quickly reveal certain outstanding characteristics. In such times, the people of God became keenly conscious of the holiness of God and of the extreme preciousness of the gospel. These truths invariably made each sin seem like a sharp stick in the eye, and the people of God could get no peace until they engaged in a thorough, profound work of repentance.

What is a thorough work of repentance? It is one that stops excusing sins, calls them by their right names, and turns from them with a true sorrow. In such times of repentance, the Christian is amazed that he could ever allow into his life things that grieve the God to whom he owes so much.

Such repentance is always painful, but when it has done its work the joy comes just as the promise says:

Those who sow in tears

Shall reap in joy

(v. 5).

Those who have studied revivals invariably make mention of the joy that comes to the people of God through repentance. There is nothing quite like it. It is the joy of walking in close communion with God, feeling his presence, knowing his approval. Revival may be likened to the heavenly Father scooping his child up into his arms to embrace him and communicate to him the deep love he has for him. Oh, the joy of that!

Verse 6 opens up another dimension of spiritual renewal. The child of God who tearfully sows the seeds of repentance over the sin in his own life will receive a bag of seed for sowing. And he is promised that his sowing of these seeds will lead to a bountiful harvest. The result of his sowing will be a great number of 'sheaves' (bundles of grain).

What are we to understand by this? Simply this—when the child of God experiences spiritual renewal, the Lord will use him in sowing the seed of the gospel to others. What greater incentive could we possibly have to seek personal renewal? Our brokenness not only brings the joy of revival, but also leads to the joy of seeing others come to the saving knowledge of our Lord and Saviour. The history of revival again bears this out. The most fruitful times of evangelism in the church have been those times when the people of God were first broken in repentance over their own sins.

The words of this psalm were written by a man who had a keen memory of past blessings and a keen concern over the spiritual decline he could see in his people. If we will stop and think for a moment, we will be able to remember times of spiritual blessing. Are we enjoying such times now? If not, let us claim this promise and begin to sow in tears.

FOR FURTHER STUDY

1. Read Isaiah 52:7-12 for another description of the joy the captives in Babylon would experience at the time of their release. What parallels can you find between this passage and Psalm 126?

2. Read James 4:1-10. What does this passage encourage in addition to lamenting our sins?

TO THINK ABOUT AND DISCUSS

1. What are some of the 'great things' that happen in a true revival?

2. Make a list of things that require your repentance. Be sure to include both the evil that you have done and the good that you have failed to do.

11 Individual thanks-giving psalms

A quick look

These psalms thank God for the blessings he has bestowed and express confidence that he will bestow further blessings. They may also be divided into individual and communal. Some of the psalms of individual thanksgiving are: 18; 30; 32; 34; 40; 41; 116.

A closer look

Psalm 30

This psalm was written by David, and, according to the heading, sung 'at the dedication of the house of David'.

We should probably take this to refer to the public dedication of the palace (the king's residence) that David built (2 Sam. 5:11-12).

This event may very well have been the occasion for David to reflect on another type of construction, namely, the spiritual re-building that had been going on in his own life.

The sobering truth is that David, spiritual man that he was, had carelessly allowed his spiritual building to fall into a state of disrepair. He leaves no doubt about the cause of it all:

Now in my prosperity I said,
'I shall never be moved'
(v. 6).

He had become intoxicated with his own success. Perhaps
it was the building of the splendid palace that made David
forget that the God who gave him all his blessings could with
a mere breath remove them. David thought he could not be
moved, but God showed him that he could.

This, then, is a psalm of chastisement. Is it not remarkable
to find it among the psalms of thanksgiving? Those who do
not understand chastisement will consider it impossible to
give thanks for it. But those who have the nub of the matter—
discipline is the Father of love pursuing his child's good—
will rejoice in it as much as David.

The psalm is comprised of the following sections:

DAVID OFFERS PRAISE TO GOD (VV. 1-3)

David is determined to lift God up in praise because God had
lifted him up from danger. In answer to his prayer, God had
prevented his enemies from triumphing over him. This
blessing from the Lord was tantamount to raising him from
the grave, which is exactly where his foes had desired to put
him!

DAVID CALLS FOR OTHERS TO PRAISE GOD (VV. 4-5)

Reflecting on his blessing made David realize that all of
God's people enjoy remarkable blessings from God. He,
David, was not alone in this. So he should not be alone in
praise.

In particular, the psalmist calls for his fellow-saints to 'give thanks at the remembrance' of God's 'holy name.'

Every blessing flows to us because God is true to his holy name. God's name represents himself or his character. God's character is such that he is kindly disposed towards his people. From that kind disposition, he has promised to bless them. Having made these promises, God must carry them out because, in addition to being kind, he is holy. If God did not bless his people, he would violate his holiness.

> Every blessing flows to us because God is true to his holy name. God's name represents himself or his character.

So every blessing God's people receive is an occasion to praise God's holy name.

The kind disposition of God is also manifested in the fact that his chastisement only lasts 'for a moment'. God's discipline can be so severe that we may be inclined to conclude that he does not care for us. But that is not the case. His chastisement, no matter how severe, does not negate his favour which 'is for life' (v. 5).

DAVID CONFESSES HIS SIN (VV. 6-7)

The psalmist gets to the nub of the matter. As noted above, he had become proud of himself. Here he sets the record straight. God is the source of all his blessings, and he, God, only has to hide his face for a moment to make David realize it.

DAVID REVIEWS HIS PRAYER FOR DELIVERANCE (VV. 8-10)

The prayer of David from the midst of the chastisement was fervent and intense. The proud heart had become the desperate heart! He had pleaded with God to spare his life so that he could live for his praise and declare his truth. This psalm is nothing less than the psalmist partially fulfilling his vow.

DAVID CELEBRATES GOD'S ANSWER (VV. 11-12)

David returns to the point with which he began. His heart is filled with thanksgiving because God had heard and answered his prayer. Those who have been saved have been chastised, and those who have been chastised are eager and ready to praise when the chastisement is over.

Psalm 32

Some burdens are so heavy that they seem to consume all our strength. No burden is heavier than the burden of guilt, and perhaps no one has ever carried a heavier burden of guilt than King David.

We know his story all too well. He—the man after God's own heart, the man who had been enormously blessed, the man who had the keen spiritual insights we find in the psalms—committed unspeakably vile and callous acts. He lusted after his neighbour's wife, committed adultery with her, and had her husband killed to cover it all up (2 Sam. 11:1-27).

THE BLESSEDNESS OF FORGIVENESS (VV. 1-2)

Forgiveness was not a light thing to David. He regards himself as being 'blessed' in receiving it. By using the word 'blessed', he was essentially saying, 'How very happy!' David was happy to be forgiven.

> But the grace of forgiveness is ever sufficient for the sin. David had found it to be so. His sin had been forgiven and covered (v. 1). And iniquity was no longer imputed to him (v. 2). God had lifted the burden and carried it away. God had covered it from view. God had blotted out the handwriting of its indictment.

If we do not share his appreciation for forgiveness, it is most certainly because we do not share his understanding of sin. Wrongdoing presupposes an objective standard of right and wrong. The Bible insists that God's law is that standard.

David alludes to God's standard of behaviour by the words he uses for his sin. He calls it 'transgression', which indicates the stepping over a known boundary. He calls it 'sin', which refers to missing a mark or a target. He calls it 'iniquity', which carries the idea of twisting something.

In each case, the thought is the same, namely, failing to live up to a standard. There is a boundary, there is a target, there is something that is straight and true, but sin steps over the boundary, misses the target, and twists the straight.

But the grace of forgiveness is ever sufficient for the sin. David had found it to be so. His sin had been forgiven and covered (v. 1). And iniquity was no longer imputed to him (v. 2). God had lifted the burden and carried it away. God had covered it from view. God had blotted out the handwriting of its indictment.

THE BURDEN OF GUILT (VV. 3-4)

The happiness that David was experiencing as he wrote these words was a far cry from that which he had experienced before he received forgiveness. It can only be called a time of agony.

After Uriah was dead and Bathsheba was 'lawfully' his wife, David thought he had successfully hidden his treacherous acts. Instead he released into his life the hounds of guilt, hounds that pursued him every waking moment and, we may be sure, even in his sleep.

David describes how it felt to be relentlessly dogged by guilt:

When I kept silent, my bones
grew old
Through my groaning all the
day long.
For day and night your hand
was heavy upon me;
My vitality was turned into the
drought of summer
(vv. 3-4).

The sense of being prematurely old, constant groaning, the feeling of heaviness, the sense of being spiritually parched and destitute—all are the handiwork of guilt.

We know about this. We have all grappled with the monster of guilt. Perhaps we cheated someone in order to get ahead, or we failed to help someone who desperately needed it. We may have failed to give the proper time to our children, or when we did give them time, we were grouchy and irritable. Perhaps we have taken God's day as our own to do with as we please or frequently taken his name in vain. It could be that we have nurtured unclean thoughts.

Or perhaps it is a combination of several things.

THE RELIEF OF CONFESSION (V. 5)

How did David get from the burden of guilt to the happiness of forgiveness? He leaves no doubt about the answer, as he says to the Lord:

I acknowledged my sin to you,
And my iniquity I have not
hidden.
I said, 'I will confess my
transgressions to the LORD,'
And you forgave the iniquity of
my sin
(v. 5).

He moved from the burden to the blessing through confession. This truth is very clear when we reduce his words to these phrases: 'I acknowledged … you forgave.'

What does it mean to confess our sins? It means to agree with God about them. Before David came to the point of confession, he and God were on opposite sides of the fence.

God was condemning his sin, and he was defending himself by rationalizing and excusing his sin.

When he finally came to the point of confession, David stopped fighting against God. He, as it were, walked over to God's side of the fence and stood with God and joined him in condemning his, David's, sin.

The relief that came to David through confession is available to all of God's people. The apostle John declares: 'If we confess our sins, he is faithful and just to forgive us our sins and to cleanse us from all unrighteousness' (1 John 1:9).

But the promise of God to forgive his repenting people must be believed. Right here is where many of God's people go astray. Even though they have God's promise to forgive them, they cannot forgive themselves. So they keep dredging up their sin and feeling guilty about it. And Satan gets the victory because, while they are feeling guilty over their sin, they are virtually useless to the cause of Christ.

What shall we say to such people? God has told us that when we repent of our sins, he casts them as far as the east is from the west (Ps. 103:12), never to be remembered again (Jer. 31:34).

Our word, then, to our troubled brother or sister who won't let go of guilt is this: dear brother, dear sister, believe God. Don't try to resurrect what he has buried. If God says you are forgiven, you are forgiven. Rejoice in it.

When we get down to the nub of the matter, it is highly insulting to God not to believe what he has said. It is, rather, sheer pride and arrogance to cling to our guilt when God has promised to forgive those who repent.

If God has pledged to forgive, we must forgive ourselves.

THE WISDOM OF EXPERIENCE (VV. 6-11)

The fact that David had experienced God's gracious forgiveness for such heinous and high-handed sins enabled him to commend confession to others. All who come truly confessing will find mercy from God. Confessing time is mercy time! David says to the Lord in another place:

For you, Lord, are good,

and ready to forgive,

And abundant in mercy to all

those who call upon you

(Ps. 86:5).

How precious is God's mercy! Those who have received it never have to worry about the judgement of God. When that judgement, like 'a flood of great waters' (v. 6), sweeps over the wicked, it will not come near those who have been visited with mercy.

So the psalmist urges his readers not to be ungovernable like a wild horse or stubborn as a mule (v. 9), but rather to avail themselves of the rich mercy of God. Those who hide in their sins (v. 5) will never be hidden in God's mercy (v. 7).

Albert Barnes summarizes this portion of this psalm in this way: 'The experience of the psalmist, therefore, as recorded in this psalm, should be full of encouragement to all who are burdened with a sense of sin. Warned by his experience, they should not attempt to conceal their transgressions in their own bosom, but they should go at once, as he was constrained at last to go, and make full and free confession to God. So doing, they will find that God is not slow to pardon them, and to fill their hearts with peace, and their lips with praise.'[1]

It has often been said that those who refuse to learn from history are doomed to repeat it. We have in David a very clear history on the matters of sin and forgiveness. If we ignore it, we doom ourselves to walk the same miserable path he walked. The course of wisdom is to learn from him, to learn what creates guilt and avoid it, to learn to confess our sin, and to learn to rejoice in God's gracious forgiveness.

Psalm 34

This psalm is usually considered to have been written by David after he escaped from the Philistines in Gath. In a fit of spiritual fainting, David had fled there to escape from King Saul. He had no sooner arrived than he heard the citizens mentioning what was said of him after he had slain Goliath. Afraid the Philistines would avenge their fallen hero, David pretended to be mad, and was driven away by King Achish (1 Sam. 21:10-15).

Later David realized that it was the Lord and not his own cleverness that had delivered him from this trouble, and he wrote this psalm.

THE PSALMIST'S INTENTION (VV. 1-7)

In these verses, David announces his intention to praise the Lord for a great deliverance the Lord had granted him. This deliverance was God's gracious answer to his fervent praying (vv. 4, 6).

After saying he will praise the Lord continually (v. 1), the psalmist here says he will praise him heartily (from the soul) and expectantly ('the humble shall hear of it, and be glad'). Regarding the latter, we may say continual, hearty worship will not go unnoticed but will gladden the hearts of other believers.

THE PSALMIST'S INVITATIONS (VV. 3,8-10)

David realized that his deliverance was not something that the Lord had done for him alone. It is a grace that God showers upon all his people. So it is fitting for David to call on his readers to join him in praise. He does so by using three exhortations.

O magnify (v. 3)

If we magnify something we make it larger or greater. The psalmist desired to make the Lord greater to all those around him. To exalt is to lift up. The psalmist desired to lift up the name of God, to place it, as it were, on a pedestal so all around might easily see it. These are glorious tasks, and the psalmist invites others to join him in them.

O taste (v. 8)

We associate taste with pleasure and satisfaction. The psalmist here calls for his readers to taste the goodness of God. Matthew Henry says: 'Let God's goodness be rolled under the tongue as a sweet morsel.'[2]

O fear (vv. 9-10)

To fear God means to live in reverential awe of who he is and to dread his displeasure. Charles Spurgeon says fearing God means: 'Pay to him humble childlike reverence, walk in his laws, have respect to his will, tremble to offend him, hasten to serve him.'³

As an incentive the psalmist promises 'no want to those who fear him' (v. 9). He points out that the young lions, the strongest beasts of prey who are most capable of providing for themselves, sometimes suffer want (v. 10). But those who fear God suffer no such lack.

This is one of those verses that seem to be patently false. It is easy for us to think of all kinds of instances in which the people of God seemed to have lacked some good thing.

We have, however, a tendency to think we know what constitutes our good. God's definition of our good is different from our own. It is for us to be conformed to the image of his Son, and all that he does in our lives or allows to happen may safely be assumed to promote that great good.

THE PSALMIST'S INSTRUCTIONS (VV. 11-22)

David was convinced that his deliverance from trouble was not a single, isolated case. He has already mentioned the deliverances of others in verse 7. Now he turns to assure his readers that they can also expect to receive deliverance from their troubles as well. The key phrase for this section is found in verse 11: 'Come, you children, listen to me; … .'

His instructions on this matter may be summarized as follows: deliverance is promised to those who are broken and contrite (v. 18) and deliverance comes in different forms (vv. 19-20).

Sometimes God delivers us from trouble after we have suffered it for a while. We want to think deliverance means we should never suffer hardship, but David clearly says we will:

'Many are the afflictions of the righteous.'

If we experience hardship for a time, and then see that hardship go away, can we not still say we have been delivered?

Sometimes God delivers us by keeping us from any real harm. He may allow us to be bruised by afflictions, but he will not allow us to be broken (i.e. destroyed) (v. 20). Charles Spurgeon writes: 'David had come off with kicks and cuffs, but no broken bones. No substantial injury occurs to the saints …. Their real self is safe; they may have flesh-wounds, but no part of the essential fabric of their beings shall be broken.'4

We are quite obviously mistaken if we expect complete deliverance in this life. That awaits the life to come (vv. 21-22).

FOR FURTHER STUDY

1. Read Hebrews 12:3-11.What does this passage teach about God's chastisement?
2. Read Luke 15:11-24.Why did the prodigal son leave home? What did he experience in the far country? What did he plan to say to his father? How did his father receive him?

TO THINK ABOUT AND DISCUSS

1.What does the truth of God's forgiving grace mean to you?
2. Why do you think it is necessary to 'bless the LORD at all times' and to have his praise 'continually' in our mouths?

12 An even closer look: Psalm 40

This psalm, written by David, is about trouble. David doesn't go into detail about the nature of his trouble, but it's clear that it was very serious. He characterizes it as 'a horrible pit' in which there was 'miry clay' (v. 2), images that convey a situation of utter hopelessness and helplessness.

We have no difficulty relating to such language. Sickness often seems to be a pit into which we sink deeper and deeper. The death of a loved one can give us the same sense, as can financial hardship and the loss of friends.

An experience of deliverance (vv. 1-10)

How it came about (v. 1)

David responded to his dilemma by waiting patiently for the Lord. In other words, he cast himself and his situation completely upon the Lord as the only possible way out. This doesn't mean he passively sat down and fatalistically said, 'If the Lord wants to deliver me, he will deliver me.' His waiting rather consisted of crying to the Lord. Prayer is the means God has ordained for working his purposes out in the lives of his children.

What it produced (vv. 2-10)

A SONG OF PRAISE (VV. 2-3,5) In due time, God heard David's prayer and delivered him from the trouble. What a deliverance it was! David's feet were lifted out of the miry clay of a horrible pit and were 'established' on a solid rock. Praise is the natural response to such a thing. This one act of deliverance made David keenly aware that God constantly thinks about his people and does many wonderful works on their behalf. His kind thoughts and wonderful deeds are too many to be counted (v. 5).

A HOPEFUL EXPECTANCY (V. 3) In addition to rejoicing over his deliverance, David rejoiced in knowing the greatness of it could not go unnoticed, that it would cause others to fear (stand in awe and reverence before God) and to rely upon him completely.

A DEEP, SETTLED CONVICTION (V. 4) David's experience caused him to state a general truth: anyone who trusts in the Lord is blessed of the Lord. Trusting the Lord is, of course, the opposite of relying on arrogant people who follow their own deceived reasoning.

A WITNESS TO OTHERS (VV. 9-10) While David knew his deliverance would catch the attention of those around him (v. 3), he wanted the glory of his gracious God to be made known to a far larger number. He, therefore, spoke of all this to God's assembled people.

We surely can't read about David's experience of deliverance without likening it to that greatest of all deliverances—that is, salvation from sin. All believers were once in the miry clay of condemnation, but God has lifted us and set our feet on the solid ground of the finished work of Christ. If David praised God for a temporal deliverance, how much more we should praise him for this spiritual and eternal deliverance!

A plea for deliverance (vv. 11-17)

David's trouble (vv. 12-15)

The horrible pit of the opening verses of the psalm is behind the psalmist, but in its place he now sees 'innumerable evils' surrounding him (v. 12). While David did not divulge the nature of the trouble from which he had been delivered, he admits that he is struggling hard against sin (v. 12). The weight of his sins was so great that he was not able to look up, and their number was more than the hairs of his head.

In addition to the keen consciousness of his sins, the psalmist was beset by enemies who desired to take his life (v. 14).

David's prayer (vv. 11,16-17)

In the midst of his despair, David, as he had done in his previous trouble, cries out to the Lord (v. 13). These verses lay before us three elements of his prayer.

HIS PETITIONS (V. 11) David specifically asks God to grant him 'tender mercies', 'lovingkindness', and 'truth'. Tender mercies refer to acts of mercy that spring from the tenderest affection. Lovingkindness is very similar. It refers to acts of kindness that spring from a heart of love. The truth refers to God's faithfulness to his promises. One can easily see how these petitions related to David's struggle against sin.

HIS MOTIVE (V. 16) In the midst of his plea, David suddenly interjects his desire for all God's people to magnify the Lord. He was not so occupied with his own problems that he forgot what was truly important. The salvation he mentions probably covers all kinds of deliverance from trouble, but we must again relate it to salvation from sin and condemnation. All those who have experienced this salvation have no hesitation about giving praise to God.

HIS HUMBLE CONFIDENCE (V. 17) Even though David found himself in a terrible state at this particular time, he was comforted by the thoughts of God towards him, and he casts himself totally upon God as his help and deliverer.

The thoughts of God! What a thought! It is astonishing that God thinks about us at all. It is astonishing that he would have as many thoughts about us as he does. It is astonishing that he thinks the thoughts that he thinks, thoughts of peace and hope (Jer. 29:11). It is astonishing that he would have the greatest of all thoughts about us, namely, the thought of eternal salvation through Jesus Christ.

FOR FURTHER STUDY

1. From the following passages, name others who experienced deliverance from God: Genesis 8:1-19; 19:29-30; Exodus 12:29-51; Esther 9:1-19; Daniel 6:13-27.
2. Read 2 Timothy 4:17-18. What kind of deliverance had Paul experienced? What kind was he expecting to experience?

TO THINK ABOUT AND DISCUSS

1. Identify some instances of God's delivering grace from your experience.
2. What is the single greatest manifestation of God's delivering grace? How should we respond to this manifestation?

13 Communal thanksgiving psalms

A quick look

Psalms of this category offer thanksgiving to God for his blessings on behalf of the community of faith. The following are some of the psalms of communal thanksgiving: 29; 33; 66; 67; 75; 106; 107; 113; 117; 124; 129; 135; 136; 147; 148; 150.

A closer look

Psalm 67

THE PLEA (V. 1)

This plea borrows the language of the priestly prayer of Numbers 6:24-26. This prayer was given by God to Moses for use by Aaron and his sons in the tabernacle worship. It came to be used regularly in the temple service. Perhaps the psalmist, finding this prayer to be lingering in his thoughts after attending one of the major festivals in Jerusalem, decided to use it as the basis for this psalm.

THE MOTIVE (VV. 2-5)

The opening words seem at first glance to be very selfish, but that impression is quickly removed when we take notice of the psalmist's reason for seeking God's blessing. It was so God's 'way' would be 'known on earth'.

John R.W. Stott explains the motive of the psalmist and his people in these words: 'They prayed that God would bless them, not in order to wallow comfortably in his blessings themselves, but in order that it might pass from them to others …. We need to remember that Israel made very audacious claims for herself and her God. She claimed to be the special people of God, with whom he had entered into an everlasting covenant. She poked fun at the dead, dumb idols of the nations. She affirmed that her God was the only living, active, and true God. So of course her heathen neighbours were watching her, now quizzically, now incredulously. They wanted some evidence to support Israel's contention. "Where is now your God?" they asked. They wanted to know what God could do for his people, what difference he made to them, whether the claims of Israel had any substance to them.'[1]

Stott adds these perceptive words about our own situation: 'It may be said without fear of contradiction that the greatest hindrance to evangelism in the church today is the failure of the church to supply evidence in her own life and work of the saving power of God.'[2]

THE RESULT (VV. 6-7)

Because the psalmist knew the gracious and merciful nature of God and because he knew his motive in seeking God's blessing was pure, he had confidence that God would indeed hear his prayer.

Psalm 117

This psalm gives no indication of its author or the occasion on which it was written. Albert Barnes suggests that it was composed for use in conjunction with other psalms. He writes: 'The psalm has no independent character of its own, and seems to have been designed, ... to be attached to other psalms as occasion might require. There is no psalm designed for public worship to which it might not thus properly be attached.'[3]

This, the littlest of the psalms and of all the chapters of the Bible, is a little gem, consisting of a fervent appeal for praise (v. 1) and grounds for praise (v. 2).

A FERVENT APPEAL FOR PRAISE (V. 1)

Here, the author reaches beyond the narrow confines of the Jewish nation to urge the Gentiles to praise God. The Lord of all should receive praise from all 'peoples' (v. 1). Barnes writes: 'This is one of the passages in the Old Testament, anticipating what is more fully disclosed in the New Testament, in which the sacred writer extends his vision beyond the narrow boundaries of Judea, and looks to the world, the whole world, as the theatre on which true religion was to be displayed, and for which it was designed. It is the language such as would be indited by the Spirit of inspiration on the supposition that the time would come when the barrier between Jews and Gentiles would be broken down, and when all the nations of the earth would be in the possession of the true religion, and would unite in the worship of the same God.'[4]

GROUNDS FOR PRAISE (V. 2)

The author gives two grounds for such praise: God's merciful kindness and his enduring truth.

God's merciful kindness

The phrase translated 'merciful kindness' by the *New King James Version* is rendered 'steadfast love' by the *English Standard Version* and 'faithful love' by the *Holman Christian Standard Bible*.

Merciful kindness! Kindness that flows from a heart that is touched by misery and need!

Steadfast, faithful love! Love that does not give up but keeps pursuing the highest good of its object! Love that will not let go! Unrelenting, stubborn love!

Which is it? Let me not choose!

Is God in truth mercifully kind? Is his love faithful and unfailing? The realm of nature says it is so. Ten thousand blessings attend us every step of our way, each blessing whispering of his love. Every thing we call 'good' flows from the fountain of his love (James 1:17).

But what is whispered in the realm of nature is shouted from the cross of Christ. There God answered once and for all those who wonder what is in his heart. It is a heart of love for sinners.

> I sometimes think about the cross,
> And shut my eyes, and try to see
> The cruel nails, and crown of thorns,
> And Jesus crucified for me.

Yet even could I see him die,
I could but see a part,
Of that great love, which like a fire
Is always burning in his heart.
(W. Walsham How)[5]

The love of God is indeed 'great toward us' (v. 2). The word 'great' is taken from a Hebrew word which is sometimes translated 'prevails' or 'overwhelms'. Perhaps the image we are to call to mind is that of a mighty flood that prevails over all or overwhelms all in its path.

> There are all sorts of obstacles and enemies between God and the sinner. But the love of God overpowers and prevails in each case of salvation.

The love of God is like that. There are all sorts of obstacles and enemies between God and the sinner. But the love of God overpowers and prevails in each case of salvation. This is astonishing love. The apostle John was astonished by it, writing: 'Behold what manner of love the Father has bestowed on us, that we should be called children of God!' (1 John 3:1).

The phrase translated 'what manner' comes from a Greek word which can be translated 'from what country'. The love of God for sinners is such that it was unlike anything with which John was familiar. The love of God for sinners is unprecedented and unsurpassed. It is astonishing love. It is astonishing that God would love guilty, undeserving sinners at all. It is astonishing that he would love as he did, sending his Son. And it is astonishing because of the greatness of the benefits which it bestows.

Elizabeth C. Clephane reflects that same astonishment in these lines:

Upon that cross of Jesus
Mine eye at times can see
The very dying form of One
Who suffered there for me;
And from my smitten heart with tears
Two wonders I confess,
The wonders of His glorious love
And my unworthiness.

I take, O Cross, thy shadow
For my abiding place;
I ask no other sunshine than
The sunshine of His face;
Content to let the world go by,
To know no gain or loss,
My sinful self my only shame,
My glory all the cross.[6]

And this love is cause for all peoples to give thanks. James Montgomery Boice writes: 'Here then is a true Christian universalism, not that all people will be saved regardless of the god they believe in, but rather that all people may be saved through Jesus Christ. To put it in other words, this is a profound missionary psalm, for it is calling on people everywhere to praise God.'[7]

God's enduring truth

Another reason to praise God is that his truth never changes.

It is not a weather vane twisting in the wind to reflect the latest opinion.

It is still true that we are sinners. It is still true that God is holy. It is still true that we cannot hope to stand acceptably in the presence of this holy God in our sins. It is still true that God has done through his Son everything that is necessary for our sins to be forgiven. It is still true that those who embrace that saving work will be saved. And it is still true that those who reject it will experience eternal destruction.

The God of truth who cannot lie has revealed these truths in his Word, and that Word, like God himself, is indestructible. The prophet Isaiah sounds this chord with these words:

> The grass withers, the flower fades,
> But the word of our God stands
> for ever
> (Isa. 40:8).

Albert Barnes states it admirably: 'What was truth to Abraham is truth to us; what was truth to Paul is truth to us; what was truth to the martyrs is truth to us; what is truth to us will be truth to all generations of the world in all lands, and will be truth for ever. *This* fact, too, is a just foundation for universal praise, … .' [8]

FOR FURTHER STUDY

1. Read Philippians 4:7-8; Colossians 4:2 and Hebrews 13:15. What do these verses teach about thanksgiving?
2. Read John 3:16 and 15:13. What do these verses tell us about the love of God?

TO THINK ABOUT AND DISCUSS

1. What can your church do to proclaim God's 'way' to the nations?
2. Think—really think!—about the saving love of God in Christ Jesus. Think about it until your heart is 'lost in wonder, love and praise'. Thank God from your heart for this saving love.

14 An even closer look: Psalm 147

hile we cannot identify the author of this psalm, we can be fairly certain about the time at which he wrote. His reference to God building Jerusalem and gathering the outcasts of Israel (v. 2) causes us to zero in on that period immediately after the captivity of the Jews in Babylon.

The psalm has been attributed to the prophets Haggai and Zechariah, who supposedly wrote it for the people to use in their worship when the temple in Jerusalem was rebuilt.

If this was indeed the case, this psalm was added to the psalter many years after most of the psalms.

The Babylonian captivity was most certainly a time of terrible heartache and anguish in which many wondered if God really cared for his people. Looking at the captivity in the rear-view mirror, and at the new temple, as this psalm does, had to remove any lingering doubts about the goodness of God.

The psalm consists of three 'sets', each of which includes a call to praise and reasons for praise.

The first set (vv. 1-6)

The call to praise is very brief and to the point: 'Praise the LORD' (v. 1). With this beginning, this psalm takes its place as the second in the 'Hallelujah' psalms with which the psalter closes (146-150).

The psalmist moves immediately from his call to praise to offer clear and substantial reasons for it.

Praise is fitting (v. 1)

Firstly, praise itself is fitting. Matthew Henry writes: 'Praising God is work that is its own wages; it is heaven upon earth; it is what we should be in as in our element. ... In giving honour to God we really do ourselves a great deal of honour.'[1]

God cares (vv. 2-6)

Secondly, the Lord tenderly cares for his broken-hearted people (vv. 2-6).

We can rest assured that there were lots of broken hearts among the Israelites during the years of their captivity. Their beautiful city of Jerusalem lay in ruins. Their glorious temple had been demolished. Their homes had been destroyed. They themselves were far from home.

The captives must certainly have found one question pounding unrelentingly in their heads: Does God care?

This psalmist wrote to answer that question triumphantly. The fact that God had gathered them home proved his care. In doing so, he had healed their broken hearts.

But healing broken hearts is not a one time thing with God. This is characteristic of him. It is his *modus operandi*.

The people could, therefore, continue to look to God for the healing of broken-heartedness.

This author sets forth an unusual treatment for broken

hearts, prescribing what we might call 'the therapy of the stars'. Immediately after telling his readers that God heals the broken-hearted, he assures them that God also numbers the stars. He could by merely looking into the night sky see countless numbers of stars. But he knew they weren't countless to God. The fact that God had them all numbered could mean only one thing:

Great is our Lord,

And mighty in power;

His understanding is infinite.

His logic is inescapable. If God was great enough to number the stars, he was certainly great enough to heal their broken hearts. He possesses both the power and the understanding to do so.

> If God was great enough to number the stars, he was certainly great enough to heal their broken hearts.

The psalmist could anticipate some of his readers objecting to his therapy of the stars: 'God numbering the stars! That only makes me feel like an insignificant speck.'

The author precludes this objection by carrying his therapy one step further. The same God who numbers the stars also has them named. He knows them individually! The implication is clear. The God who knew the stars knew his people individually. In addition to having the power to heal their broken hearts, he himself had the heart to lift 'the humble' (v. 6).

The second set (vv. 7-11)

The call to praise in this set is a bit more detailed than in the
first (v. 7). The worshippers are here urged to sing or praise
'with thanksgiving' and to do so with the harp, which was
often used in worship.

The emphasis on thanksgiving suggests that praise should
flow in part from God's kindness towards us in the past.

The reasons the psalmist assigns for praise are God's care
for the natural order (vv. 7-9) and his delight in the reverent,
trustful worship of his people (vv. 10-11).

God's care for the natural order (vv. 7-9)

As far as the former is concerned, the psalmist focuses on the
rain the Lord sends on the earth and his provision of food for
the beasts. The Lord's care goes so far as to provide grass on
the barren mountains and food for young birds that are quite
helpless.

It is easy to read the psalmist's words without giving due
thought to the care of God and how deeply indebted we are
to him for kindly providing it. Every single day we drink from
a fountain of blessings. Every day we walk a path that is
hemmed up with his goodness. When problems come we may
quickly ask ourselves why God has allowed such to come to
us. It seldom occurs to us to ask the same concerning our
innumerable blessings.

God's delight in praise (vv. 10-11)

We are also to praise God because he delights in it. The
psalmist sets the stage for this emphasis by mentioning things

in which the Lord does not delight, namely, the strength of the horse and the legs of men.

These terms take us to the military world. More precisely, they take us to two divisions of the army—the cavalry and the infantry. These things, so impressive and delightful to men, mean nothing to the Lord. Albert Barnes writes of God: 'Not in the pride, pomp, and circumstance of war is his pleasure; not in the march of armies; not in the valour of the battlefield; not in scenes where "the garments of the warrior are rolled in blood"—but in the closet, where the devout child of God prays; in the family, when the group bend before him in solemn devotion; in the assembly—quiet, serious, calm— when his friends are gathered together for prayer and praise; in the heart that truly loves, reverences, adores him.'[2]

The third set (vv. 12-20)

The final call to praise is specifically directed to Jerusalem or Zion, which was another name used for Jerusalem (v. 12). Some have taken this to mean that the psalm moves from calling all men everywhere to praise the Lord and then narrows its focus to the people of God. This is doubtful. The people of God have been in view all along. The author addresses Jerusalem merely as a way to call attention to the signal blessings that had been bestowed upon her.

What was the nature of those blessings? God had once again given security and peace to the city and the surrounding areas (vv. 13-14a). He had also given bountiful crops (v. 14b). The restoration of these blessings, after years and years of their absence, was no small reason for praise.

The author did not want to leave any doubt about the

source of these remarkable blessings. It was the powerful, effective word of the sovereign God. That word 'runs very swiftly' (v. 15). The word which goes out of his mouth is, as it were, very eager to accomplish the thing that he commands. And this word does not return 'void' to the Lord but rather accomplishes his purpose (Isa. 55:11).

The psalmist again appeals to the natural order to make his point. The snow, the frost, the hail, the cold, the thawing and the wind are all examples of the effectiveness of his word (vv. 15-18).

The people of God were enormously blessed because they had received the word of God in a special way. He had declared 'his word to Jacob' and 'his statutes and his judgements to Israel' (v. 15).

To make sure his point would not be missed, the writer says of God:

He has not dealt thus with any
nation;
And as for His judgments,
they have not known them
(v. 20).

With the concluding 'Praise the LORD!' the psalmist leaves by the same door through which he entered.

For further study ▶

FOR FURTHER STUDY

1. Read Psalm 137. What was the experience of the captives in Babylon?

2. Read Luke 4:18. What feature of Jesus' ministry links up with Psalm 147? What other features of Jesus' ministry are listed? What prophecy did Jesus' preaching fulfil?

TO THINK ABOUT AND DISCUSS

1. What does God's interest in the broken hearts of his people tell you about him?

2 What are some things that are breaking the hearts of people around you? What can you do to help them?

15 General praise psalms

A quick look

These psalms, more general than the thanksgiving psalms, seek to magnify the greatness of God. Some of these psalms are: 8; 19; 29; 103; 104; 139; 148; 146-150.

A closer look

Psalm 139

This very personal psalm (notice the pronouns 'I', 'me', 'my', and 'mine') is attributed to David. It has been called 'the crown of the psalms'. It is certainly safe to say it is one of the best loved of all the psalms and of all Scripture passages.

The whole psalm is a prayer that consists of praise (vv. 1-18) and petitions (vv. 19-24). It should not escape our notice that the praise comes first and receives much more attention. We have a tendency to rush to God with our petitions and to spend most of our time on them.

PRAISE TO GOD (VV. 1-14)

We are inclined to praise God for blessings we have received (which is right), but David praised God for who he is. Our praise will never be what it should be until we ascend to this level.

For his omniscience (vv. 1-4,6)

David begins his prayer by praising God for his perfect knowledge of him. Nothing about us is hidden from God. He knows when we sit down and rise up (v. 2). He knows our thoughts before they ever come into our heads (v. 2). He knows all about our ways (v. 3). Matthew Henry says, ' ... he knows what rule we walk by, what end we walk towards, what company we walk with.'[1]

Furthermore, he knows every word we speak before we speak (v. 4).

The psalmist stood in awe of God's knowledge. He could not begin to comprehend it (v. 6).

For his omnipresence (vv. 5,7-12)

God is to be praised because he is present everywhere. He is behind us and before us (v. 5). No one can escape from him. To drive this home, the psalmist proposes various places of hiding—heaven (v. 8), hell (v. 8), the uttermost parts of the sea (v. 9), darkness (v. 11)—but all are to no avail. By using this imagery, David is not suggesting that he wanted to escape from God (although many do), but is rather underscoring the sheer impossibility of it.

For his omnipotence (vv. 13-14)

God's power is evidenced by his creation of each individual. God created our 'reins' (our innermost being, that is, those things that control us— minds, hearts, wills). He 'covered' us while we were in the womb. The word 'covered' may also be translated 'knit' or 'wove'. By using this term the psalmist pictures himself as a fine piece of art and God as a skilled craftsman.

The psalmist's conclusion is that he is 'fearfully and wonderfully made'. Henry writes: ' ... we may justly be astonished at the admirable contrivance of these living temples, the composition of every part, and the harmony of all together.'[2]

Some of the newer translations render this phrase as a description of God—'You are fearfully wonderful', that is, a God who is so marvellous and wonderful that the only thing one can do is stand in awe of him.

It isn't all that important which of the two translations we follow. A fearfully wonderful God can only do fearfully wonderful works.

David would have us know he is not just getting carried away with his own writing. He is not indulging in poetic licence. He says it is the deep conviction of his soul that all God's works are marvellous (v. 14).

PETITIONS TO GOD (VV. 23-24)

After his long, sustained prayer of thanksgiving, David turns to make some requests of God. But his requests are not what we might expect—health, riches, peace, possessions, etc.

These things, some of which are legitimate, do not enter his mind. One cannot contemplate the glory and greatness of God without being painfully aware of one's own shortcomings. It was when Isaiah saw the Lord 'high and lifted up' that he cried, 'Woe is me, for I am undone' (Isa. 6).

We have something very similar to that in these verses.

David first asks the Lord to 'search' him for any wicked way. Sin is such a pervasive thing that we cannot even see it all. It clings to every thought, word, and deed.

Then he asks God to know his thoughts (v. 23). The word translated 'thoughts' in some Bible versions carries the idea of anxious thoughts. We can easily see why David mentions this. He has been praising the God who is unlimited in knowledge and power, the one who is present everywhere. Such a God is worthy of our complete trust and devotion. But how often we fail to trust him! How often we let anxious thoughts control us rather than childlike trust in this mighty, wise God!

Finally, David asks to be led in the everlasting way (v. 24). This is the way of righteousness. It and it alone finally leads to everlasting life. The child of God has received the imputed righteousness of the Lord Jesus Christ, and, out of gratitude, seeks to live a righteous life.

Psalm 150

The last five psalms are known as 'Hallelujah Psalms' because they each begin and end with the word 'Hallelujah', which is translated 'Praise the LORD.'

The word 'Hallelujah' is a Hebrew word which consists of 'hah-lale' and 'yah.' The former means 'to boast', and the latter is a shortened form of 'Yahweh', the Hebrew name for God. It is, therefore, a call to boast in God or to give honour and praise to God.

Although Psalm 150 is the shortest of these psalms, it is long on praise, using the term a total of thirteen times in its six verses.

After describing it as 'beautiful and animated', Albert Barnes notes: 'It was manifestly designed, whoever wrote it, to occupy the very place which it does occupy—to complete the volume devoted to praise. Praise is the suitable ending of the book; praise is what the Spirit of inspiration meant to secure in the heart and on the lips. In the review of the whole there is occasion for praise. In view of all that has been disclosed about God, about his religion, about the manifestations of his mercy and grace to this people, there is occasion for praise.'[3]

In these verses of exuberant praise, the psalmist answers three fundamental and essential questions.

WHO IS TO PRAISE THE LORD? (VV. 1,6)

The phrase 'in his sanctuary' refers to public worship on earth. The phrase 'in his mighty firmament' refers to worship in heaven. This verse is, then, in the words of John R. W. Stott 'an invitation to both humans and angels to worship God—humans in earth's sanctuary, and angels in heaven.'[4]

Having begun the psalm with a call to human beings and angels to worship, the psalmist concludes by urging 'everything that has breath' to praise the Lord (v. 6). How very often we misuse our breath! We do so when we take God's name in vain. We do so when we lie, complain, curse and gossip. We do so even when we mouth good and proper words about God while our hearts are far from him (Matt. 15:7-9; Mark 7:6-7).

The highest use of breath is sincere praise to the giver of it!

WHY IS THE LORD TO BE PRAISED? (V. 2)

The psalmist answers this question by mentioning God's 'mighty acts' and 'his excellent greatness'.

Worlds of meaning are folded into those terms! The former includes his works of creation, providence and redemption. The latter refers to God's person—that is, all the attributes that make him the unspeakably glorious God he is.

HOW IS THE LORD TO BE PRAISED? (VV. 3-5)

The trumpet, lute, harp, dance, stringed instruments, flutes, loud cymbals and high sounding cymbals (perhaps the larger of the cymbals) are to be pressed into the service of praise. Stott summarizes: 'Every conceivable instrument is to be employed in the worship of Jehovah: ... .'[5]

If we truly take up the message of Psalm 1, we will end up with the praise of Psalm 150.

FOR FURTHER STUDY

1. Read Isaiah 40:25-26 and Romans 1:20. What does creation teach us about God?
2. Read Ephesians 5:19-20 and Colossians 3:16-17. What does the apostle Paul teach in these verses about praising the Lord?

TO THINK ABOUT AND DISCUSS

1. Compile a 'praise inventory'. For what things are you praising God? What things have you failed to include? What is your praise like? What can you do to make it better?
2. What does the psalmist's emphasis on the unchangeability of God (Psalm 104:31) mean to you?

16 An even closer look: Psalms 103 & 104

Psalm 103

In this section, we look at Psalms 103 and 104 because they are companion psalms. They begin and end with the rousing, magnificent words 'Bless the LORD, O my soul.'

Psalm 103, a favourite among the people of God, was composed by David. It is pure praise, moving from David himself (vv. 1-5) to the people of God (vv. 6-18) to all of creation (vv. 19-22).

David praises God (vv. 1-5)

He speaks to himself (vv. 1-2)

David has his pen in hand. He is about to catalogue some of the many, many blessings of God that he himself has experienced.

But praise requires preparation. Our hearts, ever inclined to deadness and coldness, must be stirred to properly take up praise. If he was anything, David was a student of his heart. We all should be! So before he offers one word of praise, he stokes his heart. He preaches to himself:

Bless the LORD, O my soul;
And all that is within me

Bless his holy name!

Bless the LORD, O my soul,

And forget not all his benefits.

(vv. 1-2).

We might think modest praise is better than no praise at all. But it is not true. Modest, formal, lifeless praise is an insult to the very God it is supposedly honouring.

He speaks of God's blessings (vv. 3-5)

With his heart warmed and engaged for the task at hand, David cites some of the benefits that he had received from the Lord. There was so much in which to rejoice!

FORGIVENESS (V. 3) He first mentions the forgiveness of sins—not just some of his iniquities! What good would that be when one sin is sufficient enough to condemn before a holy God. The forgiveness of God covers 'all' iniquities. And the forgiveness of iniquities—let us never forget—flows from God through the channel of the redeeming work of Jesus Christ.

HEALING (V. 3) David moves to the next blessing: God's healing of diseases. Henry T. Mahan writes: 'The diseases of this body are the results of sin and God will heal them when it is according to his will and when it serves his purpose, but the diseases referred to here are spiritual diseases, which, like our sins, are all healed in Christ. He bore all our spiritual sicknesses and diseases in his body on the tree and by his sufferings we are healed for ever … .'[1]

REDEMPTION FROM DESTRUCTION (V. 4) David may have written this psalm shortly after a brush with death. If this was the case, he did not attribute it to luck or good fortune but to the goodness of God.

LOVINGKINDNESS AND TENDER MERCIES (V. 4) Then David adds God's crowning him with 'lovingkindness and tender mercies'. He regarded his life as having been made beautiful and attractive by the many expressions of God's kindness.

SATISFACTION (V. 5) Finally, David mentions God satisfying his 'mouth' with 'good things'. Some suggest that the word 'mouth' should be translated 'age'. The meaning, then, would be that God was sustaining David in his advancing years to the point that he, David, felt as vigorous as he did in his youth.

David calls for national praise (vv. 6-18)

In this section, David shifts from the singular to the plural as he meditates on the grace that God had shown towards all his covenant people.

Affirmation (v. 6)

The psalmist begins with a general affirmation about God's gracious character. He delights in showing grace to those who are oppressed. Showing grace to the oppressed means, of course, demonstrating righteousness and justice to the oppressors.

Recollection (vv. 7-10)

He then calls attention to a special time in Israel's history when God manifested his grace towards his people (vv. 7-10), namely, the time of Moses. When Moses came down from Mount Sinai with the law of God he found the people engaged in worshipping a golden calf. Enraged at their unfaithfulness, Moses shattered the tables of stone on which were written the Ten Commandments (Exod. 32:19). After setting things right in the camp, Moses returned to Mount Sinai with two new tables of stone. There the Lord granted him a special revelation in which he proclaimed himself to be the merciful God who forgives sin (Exod. 34:5-7).

The very fact that the nation of Israel was gathered at the foot of Mount Sinai was an indescribable act of God's grace. It was a testimony to the fact that God had delivered them from bondage in Egypt and brought them there.

Exultation (vv. 11-18)

On the basis of this slice of Israel's history, David exults in the grace of God. He glories in God not dealing with us according to our sins (v. 10). He does not deal with believers according to their sins because he has dealt with Jesus in their stead. Jesus bore their sins on the cross (1 Peter 2:24) and received the wrath of God for those sins.

> On the basis of this slice of Israel's history, David exults in the grace of God. He glories in God not dealing with us according to our sins.

Using a threefold 'as', David illustrates God's love. It is as high as the heavens (v. 11). It removes our sins as far as the east is from the west (v. 12). It is as tender as a father's pity for his children (vv. 13-14).

In addition to these things, the mercy of God is 'from everlasting to everlasting' (v. 17). What indescribably wonderful news this is for men and women whose days are so fleeting and temporary! We are as fragile as a flower. And even the slightest breeze can remove the prettiest blossom (vv. 15-16). Everlasting grace carries the people of God from fading life to everlasting glory. That grace must be called 'everlasting' because it is rooted in eternity past and issues into eternal life. In eternity past the three persons of the Trinity planned salvation. The Father chose a people for himself. The Son agreed to purchase those people on the cross. And the Holy Spirit agreed to apply the work of Christ savingly to those people.

Nothing can derail God from achieving that which was planned in eternity past. Those whom God chose will finally enter eternal glory.

David calls for universal praise (vv. 19-22)

David concludes this psalm with a fervent appeal for all the angels of the heavenly host to join the chorus of praise. Since God's throne is established in heaven and he rules over all, it is right for the creatures of heaven to offer praise.

Wherever God's dominion is to be found, praise is to be offered. Since there is no corner or crevice of the universe where it cannot be found, praise is due from all.

David traverses much ground in this psalm. He calls for praise from his own heart and finally ascends to call for praise from heaven. His trip has filled him with adoration and awe. So he drops to his own heart again and closes:

Bless the LORD, O my soul!

(v. 22).

And there we should all take our stand!

Psalm 104

Psalms 103 and 104 begin on the same note, go their separate ways, and then end on the same note. The note with which they begin and end is, 'Bless the LORD, O my soul!' (This phrase presents truths we sorely need. Firstly, God is worthy of praise from the soul. Secondly, to give God the praise he deserves, we must encourage ourselves.)

The separate ways which these psalms travel are as follows: Psalm 103 celebrates the goodness of God in salvation while Psalm 104 celebrates his greatness in creation. Psalm 103 presents God as the Father with his children while Psalm 104 presents him as the Creator with his creatures.

We can only consider the last few verses of this long psalm in which we find both reasons for praise (vv. 24-32) and the resolve to practise praise (vv. 33-34).

Reasons for praise (vv. 24-32)

God's creative work (vv. 24-26)

The key word in these verses is 'made' (vv. 24,26). In verse 24 the psalmist makes a general statement that God made everything. As he looks at creation in general, he is moved by the sheer number of God's works ('how manifold are your works!'; 'the earth is full of your possessions').

As he reflects on nature in general, he feels a sense of awe over the wisdom of God. Scientists have worked for centuries to unravel the complexities God put in place with the simple phrase 'Let there be …'

In verses 25 and 26, the psalmist moves to the sea as a

particular dimension or aspect of creation. The sea itself is not only 'great and wide', but it is filled with 'innumerable' creatures 'both small and great.'

Notable among these creatures is 'that leviathan' (v. 26). Debate swirls around the exact identity of these creatures. Some suggest the whale, some suggest the porpoise, others the crocodile. Whatever the identity of the creature, the psalmist considered it to be a special demonstration of the creative genius of God.

In addition to providing a home for its various creatures, the sea also supports a great number of ships. This not only testifies to the greatness of God but also to the smallness of man. What God holds in the hollow of his hand (Isa. 40:12), man needs a ship and several days to cross!

We need frequently to re-trace the psalmist's steps. We need to look at creation in general and say 'God made it all', and we need to look at various aspects of it and say, 'God made this.'

God's sustaining work (vv. 27-30)

The key words here are 'give' (vv. 27-28), 'open' (v. 28), 'hide' (v. 29), 'take' (v. 29), 'send' (v. 30) and renew' (v. 30). These verbs are in the present tense. God's creative work is over, but his sustaining work goes on. He supplies the creatures with what they need by simply opening his hand. When it is time for them to die, he simply takes their breath away. (The same wisdom that put all the creatures here decides exactly how long each should live. If we are consistent, we will not ascribe wisdom to God in the one and stupidity in the other.)

God's enduring glory (vv. 31-32)

It is obvious from all the things we have noted that our God is glorious in every respect. While his glory is displayed in creation, it is certainly not limited to that. One day this created order will come to an end, but God will still be glorious, and he will put that glory on display by creating a new heaven and a new earth (Rev. 21).

The psalmist draws an interesting contrast at this point. The earth and the hills are often associated with durability, but God can make the earth tremble (earthquakes) and the hills erupt (probably a reference to volcanic action) with a mere glance or a mere touch. The point the psalmist is making seems to be this: the most durable things we know are changed by God, but he never changes.

Resolve to praise (vv. 33-34)

After reciting some of the reasons to praise God, the psalmist determines that he will give God the praise he so richly deserves. Three times in these verses he says, 'I will.'

We find in these verses certain truths we may refer to as dimensions of praise. Firstly, it is to be inwardly felt ('glad in the LORD') and openly expressed ('I will sing').

Secondly, it is to be offered continually ('while I have my being'). We are not just to praise God when we feel like it or when our circumstances are just right. Here is the touchstone—as long as we have breath we are to praise him. (It also seems that the psalmist was aware of the shortness of this life and didn't want to let slip so much as one opportunity to praise God.)

Thirdly, it is to be offered with the keen desire to please God. So much of what we call 'worship' is designed to please us rather than it is to please God. How do we know what kind of worship pleases God? He has given us the answer in his Word.

FOR FURTHER STUDY

1. Read Isaiah 38:17; 44:22; Jeremiah 31:34 and Micah 7:19. How is God's forgiveness pictured in these verses?

2. Read Genesis 1:1-31. What did God create on each of the six days described in this chapter?

TO THINK ABOUT AND DISCUSS

1. What practical steps can you take to improve your praise to God?

2. How does the truth of God's unchanging nature help you?

17 Descriptive praise psalms

A quick look

These psalms can be designated as 'descriptive praise' because they describe God's character and work and offer praise for them: 33; 36; 105; 111; 113; 135; 136; 146.

A closer look

Psalm 36

Authored by David, this psalm falls in the category of descriptive praise because it both celebrates the perfections of God's character and describes some of his blessings. These themes are embedded in the larger structure of the psalm which is reflected below.

A SOBERING SPECTACLE (VV. 1-4)

Here is a psalm that thrusts before us the depressing spectacle of the wicked (vv. 1-4). The psalmist was all too familiar with it. He had seen it and had formed a conclusion within his own heart (v. 1). And the conclusions? The wicked person has 'no fear of God before his eyes' (v. 1). He conducts his life without reference to God and without reverence for him. When he looks at life and how to conduct it, he can see all sorts of opportunities to gratify his desires to do evil. But he cannot see God.

And his failure to see God leads him to flatter himself 'in his own eyes' (v. 2). How easily we fill our eyes with ourselves when we cannot get God before our eyes!

Filled with confidence in himself and assured that his way is right, the wicked person pursues a course that eventually and conclusively shows him to be the God-hater that he is (v. 2).

> Every act of mercy is at one and the same time an act of faithfulness because every act of mercy fulfils God's promise to be merciful. We must, therefore, exalt his faithfulness as much as we do his mercy.

A CHEERING SEQUENCE (VV. 5-6)

With his head still spinning from the raw audacity of the wicked, the psalmist suddenly shifts course to celebrate the mercy of God. It is not an abrupt transition. He would himself have still been within the sorrowful company of the wicked had it not been for that mercy.

But how to convey that mercy? It is in the heavens!

And the thought of mercy leads him inevitably to the faithfulness or reliability of God. Every act of mercy is at one and the same time an act of faithfulness because every act of mercy fulfils God's promise to be merciful. We must, therefore, exalt his faithfulness as much as we do his mercy.

And the thought of God's faithfulness leads right on to his righteousness. If God were to act unreliably, he would cease to be righteous. This is impossible since his righteousness is 'like the great mountains' (v. 6).

And the thought of God's righteousness requires the thought of his judgements which are the expressions of that righteousness. His judgements, especially in this context, include every act of his providential care through which he preserves man and beast.

A COLLECTION OF FIGURES (VV. 7-9)

The psalmist has gone through his sublime sequence. He is now back to mercy (the word 'lovingkindness' in verse 7 is the same word translated 'mercy' in verse 5).

That mercy is so marvellous that no one figure can adequately capture it. So the psalmist uses five.

The shadow of God's wings (v. 7)
Albert Barnes writes: 'It is not in his *justice* that we can take refuge, for we are sinners, but the foundation of all our hope is his mercy. A holy creature could fly to a *holy* Creator for refuge and defence; … but the refuge of a sinner, as such, is only his *mercy*; … .'[1] (italics are his).

The fullness of God's house (v. 8)
It is a monumental expression of God's mercy to his people that he has ordained that his house should contain a bountiful feast for them. This feast consists of the teachings of the Word of God about his redeeming love in Jesus Christ. It is a bountiful feast indeed! As believers feed on Christ, they find strength (Ps. 84:5-7), proper perspective (Ps. 73:17) and fruitfulness (Ps. 92:13-14).

But the house of God can be a place of 'leanness'. It is so when the Word of God is not truly preached, when the Word is received with unbelief and doubt, when there is dullness in hearing the Word (Heb. 5:11) and when there is unwillingness to obey the Word (James 1:22-24).

The leanness of God's house! Distressing thought!

The river of God's pleasures (v. 8)
It is likely that David used this figure as yet another way to convey God's mercy in providing his house for his people. Barnes offers this admirable summary: 'The following things, … are taught by this verse:—(1) that God is happy; (2) that religion makes man happy; (3) that his happiness is of the same *kind* or *nature* as that of God; (4) that this happiness is *satisfying* in its nature, or that it meets the real wants of the soul; (5) that it is abundant, and leaves no want of the soul unsupplied; and (6) that this happiness is to be found in an eminent degree in the "house of God," or is closely connected with the public worship of God.'[2]

The fountain of life (v. 9)
Here is another marvellous manifestation of mercy: God is the source of all that his people need for the challenges of life. From his limitless supply flows a never-ending stream of strength, wisdom and guidance.

He giveth more grace when the burdens grow greater;
He sendeth more strength when the labours increase.
To added afflictions, He addeth his mercy;
To multiplied trials, His multiplied peace.

His love has no limit; His grace has no measure;
His pow'r has no boundary known unto men.
For out of His infinite riches in Jesus,
He giveth, and giveth, and giveth again!
(Annie Johnson Flint).

The light (v. 9)

Yet another expression or manifestation of the mercy of God is his light or truth. As we look into God's Word of truth, we discover the truths we most urgently need.

A HEARTFELT PRAYER (VV. 10-12)

His consideration of the many expressions of God's mercy drives David to pray for the continuation of the same. He was especially concerned that he be not puffed up with pride, as if he deserved God's blessings. The 'foot of pride' (v. 11) always stomps out the spirit of gratitude.

And he was equally concerned that he not be driven away by 'the hand of the wicked' (v. 11). When the wicked flourish, God's people can be inclined to doubt the mercy of God. He realized that he needed to keep his head about this matter. The wicked, no matter how they seem to prosper, are already under the judgement of God (v. 12).

Psalm 113

This psalm, the author of which is unidentified, is the first of the six which are known as the 'Hallel', which simply means 'praise'. These psalms were sung at the great annual festivals in Jerusalem and by individual families in their observance of the Passover.

The psalm consists of two major parts: an appeal for praise (vv. 1-3) and reasons for praise (vv. 4-9).

AN APPEAL FOR PRAISE (VV. 1-3)

This appeal touches all the bases. Who is to be praised? The Lord. Who is to do the praising? The psalm specifically calls for praise from the servants of the Lord—that is, from those who know and revere him. He also implies by his reference to the rising and setting of the sun that all men from the east to the west owe praise to God. How long is praise to be offered? All day, every day and throughout the eternal day!

So this psalm calls for universal and eternal praise.

REASONS FOR PRAISE (VV. 4-9)

Why would the author make such an appeal? Was he allowing himself to be carried away? Was he caught up with his writing to the point of indulging in poetic licence?

The psalmist would reject all such suggestions. Consider, he says, the God to whom such praise is to be offered:

The high God

He is so high that he is above all nations and his glory is above the heavens and so high that no one can equal him or be compared to him. Furthermore, he is so very high that he has to stoop even to take notice of the things that are going on in the heavens and on earth. The heavens themselves are high above us. How much higher is the God who has to stoop to see the heavens.

The low God

The God who has to stoop to behold the heavens and the earth has been willing to do the stooping! He who is so very high has been willing to become very low.

We see this willingness every time the poor and needy are lifted to high positions (vv. 7-8) and every time the broken heart of a barren woman is healed by the joy of motherhood (v. 9). The psalmist is not suggesting that this happens to every single poor person and every single barren woman. But every time it does happen it is because of the Lord.

The psalm's emphasis on the high Lord who becomes low carries us to the gospel of Christ. The second person of the Trinity, the Son of God, was as high in glory as God the Father. But he divested himself of the trappings of his glory and became low. No, he did not lay aside his deity. God cannot un-God himself. His lowliness rather consisted in his adding to his deity our humanity. And in that humanity, he became so very low that he endured the hostility of sinners (Heb. 12:3) and went to a Roman cross where he died a special kind of death, a death such as no one before had died or anyone since. It was a death in which he endured the God-forsakenness that sinners deserve. Why did he do it? It was so he could lift those sinners from their spiritual ash heap and seat them as princes in his kingdom. It was so he could place those who are without a family into his own family.

Praise the Lord!

For further study ▶

FOR FURTHER STUDY

1. What do the following verses teach about the faithfulness of God: Psalm 36:5; 89:2,33; 119:90; 1 John 1:9?

2. Read 2 Corinthians 8:9 and Hebrews 2:9. How has God stooped to us?

TO THINK ABOUT AND DISCUSS

1. The psalmist uses five figures to convey the satisfaction he found in God's house. Write down additional figures that come to mind.

2. Think about God stooping to us in Jesus. What things about Jesus manifested lowliness and humility?

18 An even closer look: Psalm 105

This long psalm begins with the hymn David gave to Asaph and the temple choir on the day he moved the ark of God to the city of Jerusalem (1 Chron. 16:7-14) (vv. 1-5). It then moves to a historical proof of God's faithfulness to his covenant promises to Israel (vv. 6-45).

As we examine these two sections, we are able to see the psalm has great relevance for us along two lines. It first reminds us of duties that are required of all God's people, and then it gives us incentives for performing those duties.

Exhortations (vv. 1-5)

The purpose of these verses is to exhort the people of God to carry out the following duties faithfully:

Give thanks to the LORD (v. 1)

The psalmist wanted his people to realize God was the source of all their blessings and to express thanks to him. He doesn't call for them only to feel thankful, but to give thanks. Expression is necessary!

Call upon his name (v. 1)

While thanksgiving is one form of communication with God, it is only one. God's people should also petition him for their needs. Matthew Henry observes: 'Praying for further mercies is accepted as an acknowledgment of former mercies.'[1]

Make known his deeds among the peoples (v. 1)

'The peoples' is a reference to the surrounding nations. God had called the nation of Israel to be a witness to others, not simply to regard God as their exclusive possession.

Sing to him (v. 2)

God is so great that one form of praise is not sufficient. In addition to thanking him in prayer, his people are to use their voices in singing. The singing is intended to offer praise to him. It is not a matter of entertaining the worshippers.

Talk of all his wondrous works (v. 2)

In addition to talking to the surrounding nations about God, the people of Israel were to fill their conversation with one another with the things of God (Deut. 6:6-7). Another psalm puts it in these words:

> The works of the LORD are
> great,
> Studied by all who have
> pleasure in them
> (111:2).

Glory in his name (v. 3)

The name of God represents his character. While others 'glory' in such things as money, pleasure, sports, and career, the children of God are to glory in the various attributes of

God. The Lord conveyed the same to Jeremiah the prophet:

'Let not the wise man
glory in his wisdom,
Let not the mighty man
glory in his might,
Nor let the rich man
glory in his riches;
But let him who glories glory
in this,
That he understands and
knows me,
That I am the LORD, exercising
lovingkindness, judgement,
and righteousness in the
earth.
For in these I delight,'
says the LORD.
(Jer. 9:23-24).

Let the heart rejoice (v. 3)

The psalmist seems to picture the heart as wanting to rejoice in the Lord, but it is suppressed or held down by the cares and burdens of life. Our job, therefore, is not to allow our burdens so to beat us down that we seem to have no joy in our hearts.

Seek the LORD and his strength (v. 4)

The word 'seek' implies intense concentration. The call is, therefore, not to be casual and nonchalant about this matter of seeking God. In particular, the psalmist calls for his people to seek God's strength. They were to recognize their own insufficiency for the demands of living and cast themselves totally upon God's sufficiency. And let us never forget that Scripture makes a strong connection between seeking God and the sanctuary.

> God's people should be aware that his face can be turned away from them in grief and displeasure or turned towards them to smile upon them in favour and approval.

The psalmist also calls upon them to seek God's face. God's people should be aware that his face can be turned away from them in grief and displeasure or turned towards them to smile upon them in favour and approval.

Remember his marvellous works (v. 5)

It seems ridiculous to urge the people of God to remember God's marvellous works. Marvellous works would seem by their very nature to make it impossible to forget. But God's people do forget, not in the sense of being intellectually unaware that God has done these things, but rather in the sense of taking them for granted and not appreciating them as we should. Foremost among God's marvellous works is, of course, his work of salvation.

Incentives (vv. 6-45)

Who God's people are (v. 6)

The psalmist here refers to the people as the 'seed of Abraham' and the 'children of Jacob'. God's people are the spiritual descendants of these great men of God. This privilege alone ought to spur us to do the things mentioned above.

Matthew Henry writes: 'You are the children of godly parents; do not degenerate. You are God's church upon earth, and if you do not praise him, who should?'[2]

Who God is (v. 7)

He is the sovereign, mighty, and majestic God whose 'judgements are in all the earth,'—that is, he governs the whole world in wisdom and power.

What God has done (vv. 8-45)

The psalmist here takes his readers on a tour of God's mighty and merciful acts on behalf of the people of Israel. An impressive tour it is! God established his covenant with their father Abraham (v. 9) and confirmed it with Isaac and Jacob (vv. 9-10). Included in this covenant was the promise of the land of Canaan (v. 11). At the time this promise was given, their forefathers were very few in number (v. 12). The fulfilment of such a promise seemed highly unlikely! But, since the psalmist and his readers were dwelling in that very land, they knew that God had fulfilled his promise.

For this promise to be fulfilled, God had to protect their forefathers as they wandered from place to place (vv. 13-15), and this God did, as the book of Genesis testifies.

And it was God who sent their fathers into Egypt. Under the care of Joseph, they flourished there and grew into a great nation (vv. 16-24).

When God determined that the time was right for his

people to come out of Egypt, he first moved the Egyptians to enslave them (v. 25) and then raised Moses up to deliver them (vv. 26-38).

Furthermore, in the wilderness God cared for them, covering them with his cloud and providing both food and water for them (vv. 39-41). Finally, he gave them the land that he had promised (v. 44).

All of this was carried out, not because the people were deserving, but rather because God wanted a people of his own to testify to his truth by observing his statutes and keeping his laws (v. 45).

And it was all because God remembered the 'holy promise' that he had made to Abraham (v. 42).

The author's tour of history is more than mere history. The same God who fulfilled his promise to Abraham can be counted on to fulfil the promises he has made to his people today, who, by the way, are the children of Abraham. And included in those promises is something far greater than an earthly land! All of God's people stand to receive a heavenly land (Rev. 21 & 22).

We are no more deserving of that land than the people of Israel were of the land of Canaan. It is all through the matchless grace of God, grace that has been channelled to us through Jesus Christ.

Such a gracious God is worthy of praise. So let us say as David did:

Praise the LORD!

(v. 45).

FOR FURTHER STUDY

1. Read Luke 1:72. What was God about to do to show that he remembered his covenant?

2. Read Exodus 7:1-12:30. Write down in order the plagues that God sent on Egypt.

TO THINK ABOUT AND DISCUSS

1. What conclusions can you draw about God on the basis of how he dealt with Israel?

2. Take a tour of your own history. What evidences can you cite of God's hand at work in your life?

19 Imprecatory psalms

A quick look

The word 'imprecate' means 'to invoke a curse upon someone or something'. The imprecatory psalms call for God to curse or judge his enemies. While verses of imprecation can be found in other psalms, the primary psalms of imprecation are as follows: 7; 35; 40; 55; 58; 59; 69; 83; 94; 109; 137; 139; 140; 144.

Some say these psalms are merely reflections of an unworthy spirit that held sway in Old Testament times but has now been replaced with the loving spirit of the New Testament. The problem with this conclusion is twofold. Firstly, even the Old Testament calls for the people of God to love their enemies (Prov. 24:17-18). Secondly, the New Testament quotes the imprecations of the Old Testament thirteen times.

How, then, are we to understand these psalms? The answer is not in looking at them as the individual child of God seeking personal vengeance against his enemies but rather as him yearning for the only true God to triumph over his enemies. These imprecations are the prayers of those who have a consuming passion to see the cause of God triumph over all.

The following quotes provide helpful insights into the nature of the imprecatory psalms.

'Although some of them seem unreasonably harsh, a few things should be kept in mind: (1) they call for divine justice rather than human vengeance; (2) they ask for God to punish the wicked and thus vindicate his righteousness; (3) they condemn sin (in Hebrew thinking no sharp distinction exists between a sinner and his sin); and (4) even Jesus calls down a curse on several cities and tells his disciples to curse cities that do not receive the gospel (Matt. 10:14, 15).'[1]

'So, then, … it would not be right to dismiss the imprecatory psalms in the way that many do, as vindictive outbursts contrary to the mind of God, expressing the vengeful spirit which the New Testament condemns. … The truth is that what psalms like 35,58,109, and 137:7-9 are voicing is a zeal and passion for God's glory, and for the triumph of his cause and his righteousness, which far exceeds ours, … .'[2]

'It will help us progressively to appropriate these psalms and enter into their outlook if we learn to use them as prayers against Satan and his hosts, and against our own besetting sins.'[3]

'The church that is conscious of the life and death struggle between the two kingdoms will not exclude hatred for Satan's kingdom from its love for God's kingdom. The church is compelled to show love unto all men and to pray for their conversion. At the same time, with her eye fixed on the promise of the coming day of the Lord in which all God's enemies will be crushed eternally, the church prays for the hastening of the day of judgement.'[4]

'God's kingdom cannot come without Satan's kingdom being destroyed. God's will cannot be done in earth without the destruction of evil. Evil cannot be destroyed without the destruction of men who are permanently identified with it. Instead of being influenced by the sickly sentimentalism of the present day, Christian people should realize that the glory of God demands the destruction of evil.'[5]

The following words from James E. Adams take us to the central issue placed before us by the imprecatory psalms: 'You need to ask yourself right now, "Are Christ's enemies my enemies?" If they are not, you do not love the Lord as you should.'[6]

A closer look

Psalm 58

This psalm is an imprecation of David on leaders who refuse to defend the people of God. Michael Wilcock observes: 'This then is a psalm with a social conscience. It is concerned with the kind of wickedness in high places which has not only bungled or neglected those things which it ought to have done, but has also done those things which it ought not to have done—indeed, planned and perpetrated them with ruthless care.' [7]

Matthew Henry suggests that this psalm was provoked by King Saul using the vehicle of government to persecute David: ' ... he formed a process against him by course of law, upon which he was condemned unheard and tainted as a traitor.' [8]

All Christians who feel indignation at such things today

should know that they are sharing the psalmist's imprecatory spirit!

The psalm consists of four sections.

DAVID SPEAKS TO THE WICKED (VV. 1-2)

Citizens have the right to expect justice from their magistrates. But when David took up his pen to write, justice had not been carried out. The judges who were supposed to speak for righteousness had fallen strangely silent when their opportunity came. Given the opportunity to show that they were governed by higher standards, the judges had only shown that they were 'sons of men' (v. 1)—that is, men who were activated by the same principles and values that drove the mass of men.

The problem, as is always the case when people give way to wickedness, was in their hearts. They could not be right in their judgements because they were wrong in their hearts. With sin in their hearts, they could not weigh out or dispense justice with their hands but rather violence. They were rendering sentences that hurt people.

DAVID SPEAKS TO HIS READERS (VV. 3-5)

Having addressed the wicked, David takes his readers to the root of the problem. The wicked are wicked because they are born wicked. They come into this world with a sinful nature that manifests itself in both their mouths and their ears. They speak words that are deceitful and harmful (v. 3), and they refuse to listen to words of correction. In both cases, they are like snakes! In their speaking, they resemble the poisonous viper who injects its venom. In their refusal to hear, they resemble the deaf cobra that cannot be charmed no matter how alluring the music.

DAVID SPEAKS TO GOD (VV. 6-8)

The psalmist calls here for God to act against the unjust judges, using several figures to press home his point. He considers the wicked to be as vicious and dangerous as young lions. But these can do no harm if they have no teeth! So David asks God to break their teeth (v. 6).

He considers the wicked to be as dangerous and destructive as waters running at floodtide. But such can do no harm when they flow away. So David asks God to make them flow!

He regards the wicked judges as men who are armed with deadly arrows. But arrows that have been reduced to shivers cannot kill. So David asks God to shred their arrows.

David is not through. He adds two more figures. He desires God to cause the wicked to ooze away as a snail appears to do (v. 8) and to make them like a stillborn child. With the latter figure, he may very well have been referring to an abortion and asking God to abort the plans of the wicked before they can do any harm.

If we feel squeamish at David's prayer, it is because we do not see as clearly as he did the terrible heartache and havoc created by wicked leaders doing wicked things. Anyone who sees wickedness for what it is must earnestly yearn for it to end. To be at peace with wickedness is to be wicked.

DAVID SPEAKS TO HIS READERS AGAIN (VV. 9-11)

David ends his psalm with the ringing affirmation that God

will indeed judge the wicked. He was convinced that this judgement would be both swift and complete. Before the heat from burning thorns can cause the contents of a pot to simmer, the thorns are completely consumed (v. 9). So it would be with God's judgement.

That judgement would also be like a whirlwind (v. 9). Swift and complete destruction!

The point is not that God's judgement is always swift in arriving. The long history of evil shows us that it is not. It is rather that it is swift in its execution after it arrives.

Judgement for the wicked means joy for the righteous, who will wash their feet 'in the blood of the wicked' (v. 10). The soldier in battle is happy to walk on the blood of dead foes. That blood means those enemies can no longer do harm to him, his fellow-soldiers or his nation. How can he not be glad? In like manner, the righteous cannot help but be glad to see the judgement of wicked men. That judgement will mean that they can no longer do damage! Wickedness has not triumphed! The God against whom their wickedness was directed has triumphed! Who among the righteous cannot be glad?

Judgement of the wicked is essential so that 'men will say':
Surely there is a reward for the
righteous;
Surely he is God who judges in the
earth
(v. 11).

Anything less would mean that God is not righteous. And if God is not righteous, he is not God.

Psalm 137

This psalm presents an imprecation of an unknown author on those who had deeply wounded the people of God. It was written either during that time in which a large number of the citizens of Judah were being held captive in Babylon or shortly after.

The author does not identify himself, but it is safe to assume that he actually experienced both the destruction of Jerusalem and the captivity.

This is a psalm of remembrance (vv. 1-6) as well as a psalm of vehement prayer for God to remember (vv. 7-9).

THE AUTHOR'S REMEMBRANCE (VV. 1-6)

The writer had no trouble remembering. It was as if it were all cut with the point of a diamond on the plate of his mind. He remembered the weeping. He remembered Jerusalem (Zion)—once glorious, now ruined. He remembered the taunting of their captors: 'You Jews are known for your singing. Let's hear you sing now.'

And he remembered how he and his fellow-captives felt under the sting of that taunting. It was true that they did not feel like singing. But it was also true that they would not— could not!—forget Jerusalem. It would be easier to forget how to use the hand or tongue than to forget Jerusalem!

A PRAYER FOR GOD TO REMEMBER (VV. 7-9)

The Edomites (v. 7)

Although Judah and Edom had descended from the same stock (the former from Jacob and the latter from his brother

Esau), they had been at odds with each other for centuries. Even with their deep-seated hostility for Judah, the Edomites should have felt more kinship with her than with Babylon. But when Babylon destroyed the city of Jerusalem, the Edomites cheered, saying:

'Raze it, raze it,

To its very foundation!'

The Edomites serve then as a lasting emblem of all those who delight in the people of God being persecuted. If the people of God are indeed precious to him, he cannot take such hatred for his people lightly. Knowing this, the psalmist prayed for God to bring judgement on the Edomites.

The Babylonians (vv. 8-9)

This is the part of the psalm that many find very distasteful, especially the psalmist expressing the earnest desire to see Babylon's 'little ones' dashed against 'the rock'.

Some seek to soften the blow by suggesting that the term 'little ones' may not refer to physical offspring but rather to those who held to the attitude or subscribed to the spirit of Babylon, in much the same way as we speak of one being 'a child of his age'. This would have the psalmist exulting, then, not only in the prospect of God's judgement on Babylon but also in the same of all who have the mindset of Babylon.

It is likely, however, that the psalmist is rather rejoicing in God paying in kind. In the process of taking Jerusalem, the Babylonians committed unspeakable atrocities against its citizens. Babies were brutally killed and women were ravished. In taking this position, the writer was merely acknowledging the moral principle that God himself has revealed, namely, what we sow, we reap (Job 4:8; Prov. 22:8; Hos. 10:13; Gal. 6:7). More particularly, he was delighting in the prospect of that which God himself had promised to do, namely, bring severe judgement on Babylon (Isa.13:1-22, esp. v. 16).

FOR FURTHER STUDY

1. Read Matthew 26:57-68. Who are the unjust judges in this passage? What unrighteous acts did they commit?
2. Read Revelation 18:1-19:9. What lies ahead of the godless world symbolized by Babylon?

TO THINK ABOUT AND DISCUSS

1. What causes you to feel a sense of indignation, to feel that God is being dishonoured?
2. How should you pray about these matters?

20 An even closer look: Psalm 83

This psalm was written by Asaph at a time of crisis for the nation of Israel. Several of Israel's enemies had come together in an alliance for the express purpose of dismantling her (v. 4).

They wanted to divide up her land and even wipe her name from the pages of memory. Why did they harbour such animosity towards Israel? The clue is found in 'the name of Israel' (v. 4). That name represented certain things, all of which were very hateful to the surrounding peoples. The primary things, of course, were the unbending truths that there is only one true God, and that he is not to be worshipped through the works of men's hands.

The length of the list of Israel's enemies means that the conspiracy was very strong. Or are the names of Israel's most inveterate enemies collected here to reflect something of the depth of hatred of those who were generating the crisis at that time?

One thing is certain—Asaph knew what to do in this crisis! He turned to God. Do we know what to do in our times of crisis?

And what did Asaph have to say to God? We shall find four discernible threads in the fabric of his prayer.

The plea stated (v. 1)

Give Asaph credit for not beating around the bush. The situation was desperate. The people of God needed the help of their God. So Asaph begins by blurting it out:

Do not keep silent, O God!
Do not hold your peace,
And do not be still, O God!

There are times in which God appears to be indifferent to the needs of his people, times in which he seems to be lethargic and incapable of action. Every child of God could write his own page here!

Asaph was pleading with God to present himself differently on this occasion. Action was needed. God must rouse himself.

We understand, of course, that God accommodates himself to our humanness. God never grows weary, and he is never indifferent or apathetic. But he sometimes makes it appear as if he is. Why would he do such? Perhaps it is to get us to pray as Asaph did. When God seems to need rousing, it is to rouse us!

The plea supported (vv. 2-8)

Asaph could not be satisfied only to call for help. He proceeds to set forth reasons that the help was needed.

The activity of the enemies

The first was the vigorous activity of Israel's enemies. They were making 'a tumult'—that is, acting furiously and wildly. God may not be roused, but these enemies were!

The target of the enemies

A second reason advanced by Asaph is that Israel's enemies were also God's. He reminds the Lord that the hatred of these people is directed against him. God is so bound up with his people that everything that is directed against them is directed against him. That's why Asaph was able to say

> God never grows weary, and he is never indifferent or apathetic. But he sometimes makes it appear as if he is.

to God: 'Those who hate you have lifted up their head' (v. 2). Later he adds: 'They form a confederacy against you' (v. 5).

Saul of Tarsus would learn the truth of this while he was sprawled in the dust of the Damascus road. He thought he had been persecuting Christians. He discovered that he had been persecuting Christ! (Acts 9:4-5).

The nature and strength of the conspiracy

Asaph's third reason for God to act was in the nature and strength of the conspiracy. Matthew Henry says this confederacy was managed with a great deal of heat and violence ('tumult'—v. 1), pride and insolence ('lifted up their head'—v. 2), art and policy ('crafty counsel'—v. 3) and unanimity ('consulted together'—v. 3).[1]

After describing the enemy, Asaph names him! And quite a lengthy list it is, consisting of ten separate powers (vv. 6-8).

The sum of it was that Israel was no match for her enemies. But her God was!

The nature of God's people

Still another reason for God to hear Asaph's plea lies in the nature of God's people. They are his 'sheltered ones' (v. 3). This may very well refer to God obligating himself to his people in such a way that he will not allow any real harm to come to them.

The plea renewed and expanded (vv. 9-17)

Sizing up the enemy drove Asaph to renew his plea for God's help. But this time he goes into detail, resorting to the realms of history and nature to 'flesh out' his desires.

From history (vv. 9-12)

Specifically, he asks God to do for Israel the same thing that he had done in the past (vv. 9-12). He seems to say: 'Lord, do you remember how you delivered Israel from Midian (Num. 31:1-11)? Please do it again!' And do you recall how you delivered Israel from Sisera and Jabin (Judges 4)? Do it again!'

With one thought keying another, Asaph moves rapidly to the time of the judges, when God used Gideon to deliver Israel from Midian and slay their rulers Oreb and Zeeb (Judges 7). And God also used Gideon to destroy the Midianite princes, Zebah and Zalmunna (Judges 8:5,21).

From nature (vv. 13-17)

Asaph proceeds to draw three figures from the realm of nature to intensify his request. He asks God to be as the whirlwind that drives the dust and chaff away (v. 13), as the fire that consumes the trees and brush of the woods and mountains (v. 14) and as the tempest, loud with thunder and ablaze with lightning, terrifies and frightens (v. 15).

If the judgement sounds harsh to us, it is because we do not see with as true an eye as Asaph did. Serious sin requires serious judgement! And the sin was monumental. It was not merely a matter of one country being at odds with a neighbouring country over some piddling strip of ground. It was, as Asaph so plainly states, nothing less than hating God. Nothing is more vile and deserving of judgement than the creature hating the Creator and despising those who are associated with him.

We must be careful that we do not ask God to be less than we ourselves are. Albert Barnes is surely correct in making this comment: 'As all that is here sought by prayer is what men endeavour to do when an enemy invades their country, … if men can carry with them the idea that what they are endeavouring *to do* is right, whether as magistrates, judges, rulers, defenders of their country, or as private men, they will have very little difficulty in regard to the so-called *imprecatory psalms*'[2] (italics are his).

The passion behind the plea (v. 18)

If we have been inclined to think that Asaph has been speeding us towards a crevasse, we have to be relieved by this verse. He does not plunge us into the abyss of ungodly hatred. His motive is rather of the highest and noblest sort:

That they may know that you,
Whose name alone is the LORD,
Are the Most High over all the earth.

All of this has far more relevance than we may care to admit. The people of God still find that they are opposed, and the words of Matthew Henry still ring true: 'It is the secret wish of many wicked men that the church of God might not have a being in the world, that there might be no such thing as religion among mankind. Having banished the sense of it out of their own hearts, they would gladly see the whole earth as well rid of it, all its laws and ordinances abolished, all its restraints and obligations shaken off, and all that preach, profess, or practise it cut off. This they would bring it to if it were in their power; but he who sits in heaven shall *laugh at them*'[3] (italics are his).

FOR FURTHER STUDY

1. Read 2 Chronicles 20:1-30. Who prayed for victory over Judah's enemies? Who were the enemies? How did God answer?

2. Read Galatians 1:6-9 for a New Testament imprecation. Whom does Paul desire for God to curse?

TO THINK ABOUT AND DISCUSS

1. What evidences do you see of the world's hatred for the people of God?

2. What makes something a passion? On the basis of your definition, what are your passions?

21 Indirectly messianic

A quick look

These pertain to the king as God's chosen ruler. To whom do these psalms refer? Who is the anointed of God? The immediate application of these psalms is to David himself. As the king of Israel, he was chosen and anointed by God to rule.

In a larger sense, however, the kingship of David could not fulfil or exhaust all the marvellous things that are said in these psalms about the anointed. Their ultimate fulfilment must be found, therefore, in the King of kings, that is, the Lord Jesus Christ.

Some of the psalms in this category are: 18; 20; 21; 45; 69; 72; 89; 101; 132;144.

A closer look

Psalm 20

This psalm, authored by David, pictures God's people praying for and rejoicing in the victory of God's Anointed.

PRAYING FOR THE ANOINTED

The prayer (vv. 1-3) could have legitimately been offered by the citizens of Israel at any time that their king was in a crisis.

But many believers through the ages have been unable to read this psalm without thinking of Jesus' experiences in Gethsemane and on the cross. One commentator, Hamilton Verschoyle, wrote: 'The scene presented in this place to the eye of faith is deeply affecting. Here is the Messiah pouring out his heart in prayer in the day of his trouble; his spouse overhears his agonizing groans; she is moved with the tenderest sympathy towards him; she mingles her prayers with his; she entreats that he may be supported and defended.'[1]

Andrew Bonar adds: 'This psalm is the prayer which the church might be supposed [to be] offering up, had all the redeemed stood by the cross or in Gethsemane, in full consciousness of what was doing there.'[2]

> The rejoicing of the people of God is due to their being saved by the suffering of their king.

What would we have prayed for the Lord Jesus had we been able to observe him in Gethsemane or on the cross? We would have prayed the petitions of this psalm— answer his prayer (vv. 1,4a), defend and protect him (v. 1), strengthen him (v. 2), remember his devotion (v. 3) and fulfil his purpose (v. 4b).

REJOICING IN THE VICTORY

The rejoicing of the people of God is due to their being saved by the suffering of their king (v. 5). Had we been able to observe our Lord suffering in Gethsemane and on the cross, we would not only have felt his agony and sympathizingly prayed for him but we would also have rejoiced. How can such suffering and anguish be the cause of rejoicing? It was through that suffering that the people of God are saved! The Lord's suffering was not an accident or an unfortunate and unforeseen turn of events. It was the plan and purpose of God for our salvation.

The people of God in Psalm 20 also rejoiced in their king because they realized that he could be trusted (vv. 6-9). Thinking again of the Lord's sufferings in Gethsemane and on Calvary, we might be inclined to conclude anything except that God can be trusted. Those scenes of suffering might at first appear to be evidences that God the Father had failed the Son. But nothing could be further from the truth. God brought Jesus through those crises in order to work out his purpose of salvation. We can trust God, not to remove all crises and difficulties from our lives, but to bring us through them, and, in so doing, to achieve his purpose in our lives as well.

Psalm 101

The heading of this psalm ascribes it to David, but makes no reference to the occasion on which he wrote it.

This is a very personal psalm, using the word 'I' a total of eleven times in its eight verses. The pronouns 'me' and 'my' are also prominent.

It is also a prayer. The psalmist is addressing God throughout. As such, it consists of two main parts. Firstly, the psalmist looks to himself and makes certain commitments (vv. 1-4). Secondly, he looks to the citizens and makes certain commitments (vv. 5-8). In the first section, he is functioning as an individual believer, in the second, as king.

PERSONAL COMMITMENTS (VV. 1-4)

The resolutions David reports here are impressive. He will sing praises to God (v. 1), behave wisely (v. 2), walk within his house in a perfect way (v. 2), set nothing wicked before his eyes (v. 3), abhor the wicked ways of those who depart from God (v. 3), keep perversity out of his heart and wickedness out of his life (v. 4).

A fine and exacting regimen that puts most of us to shame! If we aspire to little, we shall achieve little! David aspired to much. We know he did not always succeed, but it is better to have aspired and failed than never to have aspired at all. We shall most certainly fail then!

All of David's aspirations are much needed, and there is a sense in which they all hang together—that is, we cannot really go seriously after one or two without chasing the others. But in these days of loose living in the home and loose looking—fixing our eyes on corrupt and worthless things—we may very well find David's resolutions at those particular points to be particularly appropriate (vv. 2,3).

CIVIC COMMITMENTS (VV. 5-8)

The righteousness David desired for himself is that which he desired to see throughout his kingdom. He therefore declares his constant vigilance to detect wickedness and his determination to root it out.

The other side of the coin, of course, was the twin determination to detect and reward 'the faithful of the land' (v. 6).

Because the psalm quite obviously has to do with David

and his kingdom, it cannot be considered explicitly messianic. But it is indirectly so in that David's resolutions cause us to think of the Lord Jesus Christ. In other words, one can read this whole psalm as the Lord Jesus speaking to God the Father. And while David necessarily was in the category of one who aspired but failed, Jesus is in the category of one who aspired and never failed—a category which belongs to him and him alone! (1 Peter 1:19 ; 1 John 3:5)

The Lord Jesus alone could offer perfect praise to God for his 'mercy and justice' because he, Jesus, perfectly understood them.

The Lord Jesus alone behaved wisely and in a perfect way. He alone walked within his home with a perfect heart, having never in any way sinned against his parents or his brothers.

As the perfectly righteous one, he cannot help but hate 'the work of those who fall away'.

And so it goes from point to point. But the similarity does not end with Jesus living perfectly as an individual. It also extends to his role as king over all. In that role, he most certainly will bring judgement upon all the wicked and will graciously bless and keep 'the faithful of the land' (v. 6).

For further study ▶

FOR FURTHER STUDY

1. Read Matthew 26:36-46; Mark 14:32-42; Luke 22:47-53. Describe Jesus' experiences in Gethsemane.

2. Read Joshua 24. What did Joshua ask the leaders of Israel to do? What did he commit himself to do? How did the leaders respond? How did Joshua respond to their response?

TO THINK ABOUT AND DISCUSS

1. What is there about Jesus' experience in Gethsemane that helps you?

2. What resolutions do you need to make regarding your walk with the Lord?

22 An even closer look: Psalm 45

This happy psalm was written by a man with a bubbling heart. What made his heart bubble? He had been commissioned to write this psalm about a very special event indeed—the king taking a bride.

But important as that was, it was not the reason his heart bubbled with joy. The bubbling came for this reason: as he wrote about the wedding of the king, his thoughts kept drifting to another king, the King of kings. As he was writing about his earthly king getting married, he felt himself commissioned by the Spirit of God to write about the heavenly King, the Messiah, taking a bride. And that made his heart dance with delight!

The psalm can be divided into three major parts: the reverie of the bride (vv. 2-9), the reassurance of the bride (vv. 10-12) and the presentation of the bride (vv. 13-17).

The reverie of the bride (vv. 2-9)

As she waits for the wedding day to arrive, the bride engages in deep musing about her groom. She begins with a general statement about his fairness (v. 2) which affirms that he is without equal.

She supports this affirmation by referring to his gracious words (v. 2), his might as a warrior (vv. 4-5), his enduring throne (v. 6), his love for righteousness (vv. 6-7), his fragrant garments (v. 8) and his noble attendants (v. 9). In addition to all these, she sees herself arrayed in gold and standing at his right hand (v. 9).

Believers have no difficulty seeing the Lord Jesus Christ in these details. No one is comparable to him! To use the words of yet another bride—the one from the Song of Solomon— he, Jesus, is 'the chief among ten thousand' (5:10) and 'altogether lovely' (5:16).

He speaks graciously (Luke 4:22). With his might as a warrior, he has defeated all the enemies of his people (Col. 1:15). His love for righteousness was such that he lived in perfect obedience to God (2 Cor. 5:21; 1 John 3:5). Everything about him is fragrant, especially his redeeming death (Eph. 5:2).

And his people as individual members of his bride may be regarded as his noble attendants and the whole church as his future bride arrayed in gold.

From the bride's reverie about her king, we would do well to reflect on our duty and privilege to reflect often on our Lord. The church is at her best when she is most occupied with her Lord and his glorious majesty.

The reassurance of the bride (vv. 10-12)

As the bride ponders the glory of her groom, she begins to give way to self-doubt. How could such a glorious person love her? Has she made the right decision? Will he be pleased with her?

While she is thus engaged, a friend draws near to tell her to forget her father's house (v. 10) and to assure her that she will be completely pleasing to the king (v. 11).

She must not entertain such notions. The proper response to the glory of her groom was not doubt but worship (v. 11).

The presentation of the bride (vv. 13-15)

The long-awaited day finally arrives. The king leaves his gleaming ivory palaces (v. 8) and makes his way to where his bride awaits. Her attendants rush out to meet him and excitedly announce that she is ready:

> The royal daughter is all
> glorious within *the palace*
> (v. 13).

It should be noted that the words 'the palace' are italicized, indicating that they have been supplied by the translators. In most cases, such words help us understand the sense of the passage at hand, but in this case they give a mistaken impression. The bride was not in the palace. She was at her home, and the king came to her from the palace.

The attendants proceed to assure the king that his bride is fully prepared for his arrival, that she has attired herself in clothing 'woven with gold' (v. 13) and will soon be presented to him in 'robes of many colours' (v. 14).

> The indescribable moment of meeting is followed by the procession back to the palace for the marriage feast, which would indeed be a time of 'gladness and rejoicing'.

The indescribable moment of meeting is followed by the procession back to the palace for the marriage feast, which would indeed be a time of 'gladness and rejoicing' (v. 15).

What a picture we have here of that grand day when the Lord Jesus will return to claim his bride! He will find her arrayed in the garment of perfect righteousness that he himself has provided, and he will escort her to his palace of glory where there will be gladness and joy that will never diminish.

FOR FURTHER STUDY

1. Read Ephesians 5:25-32. What do these verses tell us about Christ's love for his church?
2. Read Revelation 19:7-10. What do these verses tell us about 'the marriage of the Lamb?'

TO THINK ABOUT AND DISCUSS

1. What does the imagery of the church as Christ's bride tell you about her?
2. What does the imagery of Christ as the church's groom tell you about him?

23 Explicitly messianic psalms

A quick look

Explicitly messianic psalms do not have one level of application devoted to Israel's king and a second level devoted to the Messiah. They have the Messiah in view throughout.

We should not be surprised to find such psalms. The entire Old Testament period was one in which people of faith anticipated his coming. It is reasonable to expect that God would give his people various kinds of prophecies to fan the flame of their faith.

The psalms in this category are: 2; 22; 110; 118.

A closer look

Psalm 2

While the psalm itself contains no hint of its authorship, it is attributed to David by the apostles (Acts 4:25).

As the Lord's anointed king over Israel, David experienced opposition, but there is nothing in the accounts of his reign that answers to the details of this psalm.

We are called to believe, then, that the spirit of prophecy was upon him in such a way as to enable him to see the natural opposition that sinners have towards the Christ of God.

THE RULERS SPEAK TO ONE ANOTHER (VV. 1-3)

This psalm begins abruptly with a scene of profound turbulence and turmoil. The nations of the earth and their kings are pictured as raging against persons in authority. They meet together to plot the overthrow of these persons (v. 2), crying:

> Let us break their bonds in
> pieces
> And cast away their cords
> from us
> (v. 3).

Who is the object or focus of such virulent opposition? The psalmist leaves no doubt. It is directed against 'the LORD' and 'his anointed' (v. 2).

THE PSALMIST SPEAKS ABOUT THE LORD (VV. 4-5)

Hate all they want, plan all they like, fret and fuss all they wish, men can never rid themselves of God. Hostility is futile. Why? God is sovereign. He sits in heaven. In other words, he transcends men. He is far superior. And how does this scene of raging hostility strike him? Is he stricken with terror? Does he fly into a panic? Does he call an emergency session of the heavenly cabinet? No. He just laughs. He scoffs at puny men as they parade briefly across the stage of history, as they fume and fuss (v. 4).

After laughing, God speaks:

> Yet I have set my king
> On my holy hill of Zion
> (v. 6).

The Lord God has already done the very thing his enemies most want to prevent. He has already made Christ King. Charles Spurgeon writes: 'While they are proposing, he has disposed the matter. Jehovah's will is done, and man's will frets and raves in vain. God's Anointed is appointed, and shall not be disappointed.'[1]

THE ANOINTED SPEAKS TO THE RULERS (VV. 7-9)

At this juncture the Anointed one himself, Jesus Christ, speaks. His words take us back to the moment when God decreed that he should reign. There was a time even before this world existed, when the triune God planned the redemption of sinners. At that time the Second Person of the Trinity agreed to take unto himself human flesh in 'the fullness of time' (Gal. 4:4).

At that point the Father said to the Son: 'You are my Son; Today I have begotten you' (v. 7). God anointed Christ then to become king through the work of redemption, and no one can ever change it.

As the Anointed continues to speak, he reveals that which God will yet do. This one who has been anointed as God's king will someday receive all nations as his inheritance and the ends of the earth as his possession (v. 8). In other words, he will eventually enjoy absolute dominion, and those who resist will be crushed by his power (v. 9; 1 Cor. 15:24-28; Phil. 2:9-11).

> Jesus shall reign where'er the sun
> Does his successive journeys run;
> His kingdom spread from shore to shore,
> Till moons shall wax and wane no more.

The psalm concludes with David counselling the opposers of
Christ. If hostility is futile, the only reasonable thing for men
to do is throw down their arms and submit to God. His
injunctions are swift and abrupt.

'Be wise' (v. 10) means to think this thing out. Recognize
the situation for what it is. Don't nurse hope of succeeding
against God.

'Serve the LORD with fear' (v. 11) means to worship God.
Recognize God's greatness and bow in awe before him.

'Rejoice with trembling' (v. 11) means that in submitting to
God we shall find our true happiness and joy. We might think
serving the Lord is a miserable thing, but it's really the
greatest joy we can ever have. If we would only recognize this
we would be more willing to cease our rebellion.

'Kiss the Son' (v. 12) means to show him homage and true
affection. The admonition is to cease hating God's king and
start loving him.

What about those who refuse to submit, continuing in
their hostile rebellion? Verse 12 gives the answer:

Kiss the Son, lest he be angry,

And you perish in the way,

When his wrath is kindled but

a little.

The option is clear. Those who refuse to submit will
someday be cut off while they are still walking 'in the way' of
rebellion. They will be going along in their hatred, spewing
out their venom against God, and he will step in, cut them
off, and send them into eternal destruction. In short, we are

presented with this option concerning Christ: cherish or perish!

> Ye sinners seek his grace,
> Whose wrath ye cannot bear;
> Fly to the shelter of his cross,
> And find salvation there.[2]

Psalm 110

Which psalm is most quoted by the New Testament authors? It is not the ever-popular twenty-third Psalm. Some might think the answer is the very long Psalm 119, which offers more to quote. It is Psalm 110. Its first verse is referred to one way or another a total of twenty-seven times in the New Testament.

This psalm certainly belongs in the category 'explicitly messianic'. Evangelical commentators are virtually agreed that this psalm does not rise from the reign of an earthly king to the Messiah, as do the psalms in the 'indirectly messianic' category. It begins and ends with the Messiah. It is David expressing his faith in the Messiah. Matthew Henry states: 'This psalm is pure gospel; it is only, and wholly, concerning Christ, the Messiah promised to the fathers and expected by them.'[3]

Albert Barnes agrees: 'The application of the psalm in the New Testament to the Messiah is so clear and unequivocal, that we are bound to defend the opinion that it was designed to refer to him; and the manner in which it is quoted shows ... that it had an original and exclusive applicability to him.'[4]

This psalm reminds us, then, of the essential nature of the faith of the Old Testament saints. They were not saved by keeping the law of Moses, but rather in the very same way as people today, namely, through faith in Jesus Christ. The only difference between their faith and ours is that theirs looked forward to the coming Christ, while ours looks back to the Christ who has come.

This psalm also shows us that there is in the Old Testament such a thing as prophecy. David and others wrote centuries in advance about the Christ and his redeeming work, and their writings were fulfilled to the letter by the Lord Jesus.

The psalm reports the words of two speakers. There is no doubt about the identity of the first. It is none other than God himself. And there is no doubt about the one to whom he was speaking. It was the Messiah (vv. 1-4).

The mystery sets in with the identity of the second speaker (v. 5). Is he, as some have suggested, the Messiah? If so, to whom is he speaking? Is he answering the Father? Or is he speaking to his people? Or do we have the psalmist responding to the Father's words about the Messiah?

We cannot be one hundred per cent sure, but it seems likely that the latter is the case. And that is the approach we will take.

THE FATHER SPEAKS TO THE SON (VV. 1-4)

A sense of wondering awe must have been upon David as he wrote these words. He is reporting words spoken by the Lord to the Lord! Of course, he had not been present in the eternal councils of God to hear these words. He is able to write them only because the Spirit of God revealed them to him.

Who are these Lords (v. 1)? The first 'LORD' refers to

Jehovah, the second ('Adonai') to one who is in authority or has dominion.

David is affirming that the Lord God had spoken to one who had authority or dominion over him, that is, over David. Who was this person? David was king of all Israel. Who had authority over him? It was none other than the Second Person of the Trinity, the Son of God and the coming Messiah!

What a unique and delectable position David enjoyed! God had promised that the Messiah would physically descend from him. So the Messiah would be his son. But that same Messiah would be far more than a mere man. He would at one and the same time be God and man. The God-man! God in human flesh! So David's son would also be his Lord!

> But that same Messiah would be far more than a mere man. He would at one and the same time be God and man. The God-man! God in human flesh!

The Lord Jesus must have enjoyed discomfiting the Pharisees with that one! (Matt. 22:41-45).

And what did the Lord (Jehovah) have to say to David's Lord, the Messiah? He spoke of his reign and the success of it. This is the gospel reign of Jesus, the reign in which he is even now engaged. Having completed the work of redemption and having ascended to heaven, he is even now at the right hand of God—the position of honour and rank. There are several things for us to note about this reign from this psalm:

Complete subjection
This reign will result in the complete subjection of all the Messiah's enemies (v. 1). Every knee will finally bow before him and every tongue will finally confess that he is Lord (Phil. 2:9-11).

Present success
This reign is even now conquering enemies. As the church preaches the gospel, the Lord Jesus Christ extends his 'rod' or sceptre 'out of Zion'.

Present evidence
This reign is evidenced by the people of God themselves (v. 3). They were once among the enemies of Christ. But the gospel conquered them. How were they conquered? By being made willing to receive the gospel! Thus the Father says to the Messiah:

> Your people shall be volunteers
> In the day of your power;

Walter Chantry concludes: 'The army of Christ has never conscripted its troops. Each one has been mysteriously, secretly made willing in the depths of his being.'[5]

Albert Barnes adds: 'There is no compulsion in his religion. Men are not constrained to do what they are unwilling to do. All the power that is exerted is on the will, disposing men to do what is right, and what is for their own interest. No man is forced to go to heaven against his will; no man is saved from hell against his will; no man makes a sacrifice in religion against his will; no man is compelled to serve the Redeemer in any way against his will.'[6]

The gospel which has operated in these people did so with the purpose of securing 'the beauties of holiness' from them, and that holiness gives evidence of the gospel.

Future success

These people are not few in number. The gospel will perform so effectively that the people of the Lord will finally prove to be as numerous as the drops of dew that come 'from the womb of the morning'.

The basis

The gospel reign has as its centrepiece the priestly work of the Lord Jesus Christ. The king is also a priest! He is a priest by virtue of the appointment of the one who does not change his mind and whose word cannot be overturned.

In his priestly work, the Lord Jesus is from 'the order of Melchizedek', the king-priest of Abraham's day (Gen. 14:18-20). Melchizedek was both 'king of righteousness' (which is the meaning of his name) and 'king of peace' (which is the meaning of Salem, the city where he ruled, the city which would later be known as Jerusalem).

While Melchizedek could only imperfectly represent these things, Jesus is truly the king of righteousness and peace. And the way by which he produced peace between guilty sinners and the holy God was through righteousness. He himself lived a perfectly righteous life, providing the righteousness that we do not have, righteousness that is credited to us when we believe. Furthermore, Jesus' death also had to do with righteousness. He died to receive the righteous sentence of the holy God against our sins. In other words, he received on the cross what God's righteousness demanded, namely, the wrath of God.

Melchizedek also represents a continuing, eternal priesthood. The fact that no genealogy is given for him makes it appear that he had no parents and suggests endlessness (Heb. 7:3). While Melchizedek could only suggest or represent endlessness, the Lord Jesus actually possesses it. His priesthood, in which he represents sinners before God, will continue for ever.

Furthermore, as Melchizedek pronounced a blessing upon Abram (Gen. 14:19-20), the Lord Jesus Christ, the priest of his people, pronounces blessing upon them as well. All spiritual blessings flow to us, not because of anything we do to earn or deserve them, but solely because of the priestly work of Christ on our behalf.

THE PSALMIST SPEAKS TO THE FATHER (VV. 5-7)

Having heard the Father speak to the Son about the gospel reign, David responds. Under the spirit of prophecy, he, David, is able to see the Messiah's judgement upon those who reject him. In these verses, he confesses the truth of this coming judgement. He essentially says to God: 'By the power of your spirit, I now understand that the Lord whom you have placed at your right hand will judge his opposers.'

Severe

This judgement will be severe. The word 'execute' translates a word that refers to shattering or dashing to pieces. It will be the type of day that truly earns the title 'the day of his wrath' (v. 5). It will be the day in which he will fill the hollow places of the earth with 'dead bodies' (v. 6).

Some try to remove the sting of such language by pointing out that it is figurative. But what kind of reality is it that requires such language to convey it? The Bible teaches that the divine judgement these terms were meant to express is a most fearful and dreadful reality indeed.

Thorough

This judgement will be thorough. Even kings (v. 5) and 'the heads' of countries (v. 6) will not be too great to escape it. It will go through the nations (v. 6).

Unfailing

This judgement will be completed. It will not fail through lack of determination or vigour on the part of the Messiah. We often undertake a work only soon to lay it aside because of weariness or lack of interest. But the Messiah will not give up the work of judgement until it is done. The psalmist says of the Messiah:

He shall drink of the brook by
the wayside;
Therefore he shall lift up the
head
(v. 7).

Our heads droop when we are exhausted. But the Lord Jesus will be like a warrior who, in the process of pursuing his fleeing enemies, comes to a stream and drinks. Refreshed, he continues his pursuit and overtakes his enemies.

The teaching of this psalm echoes that of Psalm 2. The Lord Jesus is God's appointed king who will win the victory over us either by making us willing to receive his salvation or by bringing us under his judgement. Either way he will have his victory.

FOR FURTHER STUDY

1. Read Matthew 22:41-45. What is the first question Jesus asked the Pharisees in these verses? How did they answer? What is the second question Jesus asked? How did the Pharisees respond?
2. Read Revelation 20:11-15. What does this passage teach about the final judgement?

TO THINK ABOUT AND DISCUSS

1. How does God's decree that Christ shall rule bring encouragement to you?
2. Discuss the gospel reign with some friends. What does it mean? What are the evidences of it? How should we be responding to it?

24 An even closer look: Psalm 22

Here David lifts up his eyes, looks down the long corridor of time, and sees in striking detail the crucifixion of the Messiah who was yet to come.

We have to call this a psalm of prophecy—even as the apostle Peter referred to Psalm 132 as a psalm of prophecy (Acts 2:30-31)—because we can find nothing in David's life that would require the language he uses in these verses and because we do find the cross of Christ answering detail after detail of the psalm.

Some have suggested that this prediction of the cross is so exact that it makes us think it had to be written by one standing at the foot of the cross. But this is not the psalm of an observer reporting an event. It was written almost a thousand years before the event, and it is written in the first person. Here we have one telling about his own experience. We have to say, therefore, that this psalm is the result of the Spirit of God taking over the pen of David in a strange and marvellous way so he, David, was able

> Some have suggested that this prediction of the cross is so exact that it makes us think it had to be written by one standing at the foot of the cross.

to write the very words of the Messiah himself.

The psalm falls into two easily discernible sections. The first is the Messiah's description of the crucifixion (vv. 1-21a). The second is his description of the results of the crucifixion (vv. 21b-31). We might say the psalm is divided between the Messiah's experience on the cross and his exultation in the results of the cross.

The experience of the Messiah on the cross

The description in these verses leaves no doubt that the crucifixion of Christ is in view here.

The words Jesus spoke from the cross are here

Firstly, some of the words Jesus spoke from the cross are either stated or suggested here. The abrupt opening of the psalm takes us to the very words Jesus spoke when darkness shrouded the land: 'My God, My God, why have you forsaken me?' (Matt. 27:46).

The reference to the tongue clinging to the jaws (v. 15) makes us think of Jesus' cry, 'I thirst!' (John 19:28).

The very last words of the psalm, which are probably best translated 'he has done it', make it very difficult for us not to think of Jesus' triumphant cry: 'It is finished!' (John 19:30).

The reason Jesus was on the cross is here

After the opening cry of this psalm, the psalmist takes us to the reason for it. It is right there in that phrase:

But you are holy, …

(v. 3).

Jesus cried out, 'My God, My God, why have you forsaken

Me?' for a very simple and obvious reason. He was forsaken of God while he was there on the cross. And why was he forsaken of God? He was taking the place of sinners. He was 'made' sin for those whom the Father had given him before the foundation of the world (2 Cor. 5:21). He was bearing their penalty.

The ultimate penalty for sin is God-forsakenness for ever. It is to be separated from God in that place of eternal destruction, hell (2 Thes. 1:9). In order for Jesus to bear that penalty he had to be forsaken of God.

We have never begun, even in our moments of keenest insight, to understand the depths of Calvary. There the Lord Jesus Christ bore in his own person an eternity of the wrath of God. He, being infinite, suffered in a finite amount of time what we, being finite, would suffer in an infinite amount of time. Eternity was compressed upon him.

Why did he do it? The holiness of God demanded it. The prophet Habakkuk was right. God is of 'purer eyes' than to behold evil (Hab. 1:13). In that awesome period in which Jesus actually became the sin-bearer, the holy God withdrew from him. God forsaking God! That is the essence and the unfathomable depth of the cross. And it is all clearly foretold in this psalm.

During that time of God-forsakenness, a deep darkness fell over the land (Matt. 27:45). One is tempted to see in the psalmist's phrase 'in the night season' (v. 2) a prophecy of that deep darkness.

The sufferings Jesus endured on the cross are here

The mockery and ridicule Jesus received are foretold here.

The psalmist says:

> But I am a worm, and no man;
> A reproach of men, and
> despised by the people.
> All those who see me ridicule
> me;
> They shoot out the lip,
> they shake the head, saying,
> 'He trusted in the LORD,
> let him rescue him;
> Let him deliver him,
> since he delights in him!'
> (vv. 6-8).

How exactly this corresponds to what we find in Matthew 27:41-43:

> Likewise the chief priest also, mocking with the scribes and elders, said, 'He saved others; himself he cannot save. If he is the King of Israel, let him now come down from the cross, and we will believe him. He trusted in God; let him deliver him now if he will have him; for he said, "I am the Son of God."'

In addition to the mockery, this psalm, as noted above, predicts the thirst of Christ. In his description of the crucifixion, the apostle John notes this thirst was a fulfilment of prophecy (John 19:28).

We even find the word 'pierced' in Psalm 22, a word that is associated with crucifixion. (The Geneva Study Bible points out that the traditional Hebrews rendering, 'like a lion' probably reflects a copyist's error. The Septuagint, which is the ancient Greek translation of the Old Testament, uses the word 'pierced'.)[2]

The significant point is that David wrote this psalm long before crucifixion was even adopted as a means of execution.

This psalm also prophesies the dividing of Jesus' garments, a prophecy that Matthew notes was minutely fulfilled (Matt. 27:35).

Those who crucified Jesus are here

Who was it that crucified Jesus? The Roman soldiers? Yes. The Sanhedrin? Yes. But pre-eminently it was God who crucified the Lord Jesus Christ.

Psalm 22 contains hints of the involvement of the Romans (the word 'dogs' in verse 16 was the Jewish way of referring to Gentiles) and the Jews ('the congregation' or 'assembly' of the wicked in verse 16 may very well refer to the Sanhedrin).

But the hand of God is not hinted at in this psalm. It is explicitly stated in these words spoken to God:

You have brought me to the
dust of death
(v. 15).

The precision of this statement is borne out by other Scriptures. The apostle Paul says God 'set forth' his Son as a 'propitiation' for our sins (Rom. 3:25). It was God who refused to spare his Son, but rather 'delivered him up for us all' (Rom. 8:32). It was God who was 'pleased' to 'bruise' the Lord Jesus and put him to 'grief' (Isa. 53:10). Yes, it was God who sent his Son to the cross.

All these things amount to a mere scratch of the surface, but they should convince us that this psalm is indeed saturated with the cross of Christ.

The Messiah's exultation in the results of the cross

Verse 21 brings us to a turning point in the psalm. The darkness lifts and the sunshine beams brightly. The storm of wrath has subsided and all is peaceful and calm.

In the verses that remain the Messiah rejoices that his death on the cross was not in vain, but that it achieved its purpose. Because of that death he now has 'brethren' to whom the name of God can be declared (v. 22). The author of Hebrews relates this portion of the psalm to all those who know the Lord Jesus Christ as their Lord and Saviour. He says Christ is 'not ashamed' to call those who know him his 'brethren' (Heb. 2:10-12).

Furthermore, because of his death on the cross the Messiah rejoices in the poor being able to eat and be satisfied (v. 26). What a marvellous picture this is of sinners coming to know the crucified redeemer! Because of his death they can eat of the gospel feast and be satisfied with the knowledge their sins are forgiven and they can, therefore, stand without fear in the presence of the holy God.

The Messiah also rejoices in 'all ends of the earth' turning to him. His death on the cross was not just for one nation but for people of all nations, and it will finally issue in the redemption of a multitude.

... Out of every tribe and tongue

and people and nation, ...

(Rev. 5:9).

The Messiah rejoices still further in the fact that his death will also issue in the final vindication of God. He says:

And all the families of the
nations
Shall worship before you
(v. 27b).

This certainly brings to mind the words of the apostle
Paul: ' ... at the name of Jesus every knee should bow, of
those in heaven, and of those on earth, and of those under the
earth, and that every tongue should confess that Jesus Christ
is Lord, to the glory of God the Father' (Phil. 2:10-11).

Finally, the Messiah rejoices in the knowledge that 'a
posterity' will serve him. Each generation will have those
whom he purchased with his own blood to tell those in the
generation following them of what he has done (vv. 30-31).

So Jesus did not die on the cross with his fingers crossed
that what he was doing would somehow accomplish
something. That cross that he and the Father agreed upon
before the world began would be effective in redeeming the
Father's love gift. That cross was adopted in eternity past as
the only means of salvation. It was announced in Eden, and,
as Psalm 22 clearly reveals, the Father and the Son never
detoured from that cross throughout the Old Testament
period. It was ever in their view.

For further study ▶

FOR FURTHER STUDY

1. Read Isaiah 53. In what ways did Jesus' death on the cross fulfil this prophecy?
2. Read 1 Corinthians 2:2 and Galatians 6:14. What was Paul's attitude towards the cross?

TO THINK ABOUT AND DISCUSS

1. What truths about the cross of Christ are most precious to you?
2. Discuss with others your understanding of the cross and ask them to do the same with you.

25 Enthronement psalms

A quick look

These psalms describe God's sovereign and unending rule over all creation. The following psalms are generally placed in this group: 15; 24; 47; 93; 96-99.

A closer look

Psalm 47

This is one of twelve psalms with this heading: 'To the Chief Musician. A Psalm of the sons of Korah.'

The name Korah is a familiar—and unsavoury—one. He was in the forefront of those who rose up in rebellion against Moses and paid for it with their lives (Num. 16).

But good shoots sometimes sprout from rotten stock. So it was with Korah. Some of his descendants became singers and musicians in the Levitical or temple choir, which was established by David.

This psalm apparently was written by the choir director for the sole purpose of expressing delight in the rule of God. Derek Kidner puts it in these words: 'From the first word to the last, this communicates the excitement and jubilation of an enthronement; and the king is God Himself.'[1]

We can well imagine that the descendants of Korah took pleasure in singing a truth that their family history so fully and sadly demonstrated. God rules! That the choir members knew right well from their forefather Korah.

The psalm vibrates with joy through two 'festive bursts', each of which begins with a ringing exhortation to praise (vv. 1,6) and moves to plain reasons for doing so (vv. 2-5,7-9).

THE FIRST FESTIVE BURST (VV. 1-5)

The opening exhortation shows us that praise to God should be exuberant and heartfelt.

Anything less, as the following reasons show (vv. 2-5), does not do justice to the God to whom it is supposedly directed.

It is likely that this psalm was composed to celebrate a military victory of Israel. Such a victory served as indisputable proof that God was awesome (v. 2) and 'a great King over all the earth' (v. 2). It was also to be taken as a token that God would continue to subdue Israel's enemies (v. 3) and would continue to choose Israel's land as her inheritance (v. 4). Furthermore, it proved God's love for his people (v. 4).

As far as the Israelites were concerned, this military conquest was as if God had come down from heaven to help and then had returned there with a shout of triumph and with the blasts of a trumpet (v. 5).

Minimal blessings would make minimal praise fitting, but great blessings from the great God call for great praise (Ps. 48:1).

Believers in Christ have no difficulty finding parallels between this psalm and the gospel of Christ. The gospel means that God has come down to this earth, defeated Satan on their behalf and returned to heaven in triumph. All of this was done, of course, through the coming, the living, the dying, the rising and the ascending of the Lord Jesus Christ.

THE SECOND FESTIVE BURST (VV. 6-9)

The psalm calls again for praise with these words:

Sing praises to God, sing praises!

Sing praises to our King, sing praises!

(v. 6).

The reasons advanced in this section are similar to those in the first. God has demonstrated that he is 'the King of all the earth' (v. 7), that he 'reigns over the nations' (v. 8) and 'sits on his holy throne' (v. 8).

> Minimal blessings would make minimal praise fitting, but great blessings from the great God call for great praise.

God's might in defeating Israel's enemy had been displayed for all to see. The princes, that is, leaders of the conquered nation had been 'gathered', and along with their shields, had been paraded before 'the people of the God of Abraham' (v. 9) in a triumphant victory celebration.

One difference between the second section of praise and the first is that the former includes the phrase: 'Sing praises with understanding' (v. 7). Albert Barnes offers this explanation: 'The idea is, that the occasion was one on which *such* a psalm or song would be peculiarly appropriate; an occasion on which great *lessons* or *truths* had been taught by the dealings of God, which it became his people now to set forth in a becoming manner. Those lessons or truths pertained to the fact that God is the great King over all the earth, or that he is a sovereign among the nations—a truth of immense importance to mankind, and a truth which the occasion on which the psalm was composed was peculiarly adapted to bring to view' [2] (italics are his).

Psalm 93

This is the first of a cluster of the enthronement psalms. Some suggest this cluster consists of Psalms 93-100.

Three of these psalms 'nail their colours to the mast' with their opening words: 'The LORD reigns' (93:1; 97:1; 99:1).

The author of Psalm 93 does not give us his name or his reason for writing.

While we cannot connect the psalm with a specific situation or set of circumstances in the nation of Israel, we can, as it were, work back from what the psalm says to construct something of what was going through the author's mind.

The term 'the floods' may very well be a key (v. 3). Martin Luther spoke of 'the flood of mortal ills prevailing'. One wonders if the psalmist was not keenly conscious of the same.

Albert Barnes, I think, has captured the mood that gave birth to this psalm: 'It would appear as if the psalmist had been meditating on dark things which occur in the world; the mysteries which abound; the things which seem irreconcilable with the idea that there is a just government over the world, ...'[3]

If that was indeed the case, this is a psalm for today.

One thing is for sure: mortal ills, when they prevail, make it look as if God is not in charge, or, if he is, he is performing very poorly.

Perhaps the psalmist, amid his own flood of mortal ills, found himself giving in to the suggestion that the world is throne-less, or, to change the figure, rudder-less.

God has testified that this is not the case. God has testified that he is sovereign and in control and that when it appears as if he is not, it is in appearance only.

But when the flood of ills rises higher and higher, many rush to the forefront, grab the microphone and announce to the beleaguered that the testimonies of God are not true. And when the tide is particularly high, the microphone becomes a megaphone.

In better times, the psalmist had come to the truth of the matter, and here he states it—The Lord reigns! It is always good when we are in the dark to hold on to what we saw in the light.

So the psalmist gets in his opportunity, saying:

THE LORD DOES REIGN (V. 1) Take God out of the picture. Now what do we have? We still have the mortal ills. That's for sure. And they often run at floodtide. But what else do we have? Nothing at all. With God removed, all we have is the flood. We do not have all the answers with God, but we have none without him. It is better to have some answers with the promise of having all the answers than it is to have none at all.

THE LORD IS CLOTHED IN MAJESTY AND STRENGTH (V. 1) Could it possibly be that such a glorious God has purposes that are far beyond our ability to comprehend and that through our flood of ills he accomplishes those purposes? How can the parent explain to the infant that the surgery he needs is not to destroy his health but to secure it?

THE LORD HAS ESTABLISHED THE WORLD, and it cannot be destroyed by any or all mortal ills (v. 1)

THE LORD GOD AND HIS THRONE OR RULE ARE EVERLASTING and cannot be affected or moved by any or all of the turbulence of life in this world (v. 2)

THE LORD IS HIGHER than the highest tide of the ills (vv. 3-4)

THE TESTIMONIES OF THE LORD ARE TRUE (V. 5) The storms of life may very well suggest otherwise. But God has demonstrated again and again that his word can be trusted. In the end, it will be plain to all that not one of God's testimonies has failed in any respect. We would do well, then, to go back to Martin Luther, taking these words as our own:

That word above all earthly powers,

No thanks to them, abideth;

The Spirit and the gifts are ours

Thro' Him who with us sideth:

Let goods and kindred go,

This mortal life also;

The body they may kill:

God's truth abideth still,

His kingdom is for ever.

THE LORD'S HOUSE IS A GOOD REFUGE IN THE FLOOD (V. 5) Let us never be in doubt that the flood of ills is due to one thing and one thing only—sin. But there in the flood stands the church of the living God. There she stands to maintain the principles of holiness in a world that is awash in sin. And there flood-weary people may go to find refuge.

FOR FURTHER STUDY

1. Read Numbers 16. What complaint did Korah and those with him lodge against Moses? How did Moses respond? What form did God's judgement take?

2. Read 2 Corinthians 4:7-16. What 'mortals ills' does Paul list here? In what truths did he find strength?

TO THINK ABOUT AND DISCUSS

1. What do you think it means to 'sing praises with understanding' (Ps. 47:7)?

2. Make a list of some of your ills. What practical steps can you take to remind yourself of God's sufficiency?

26 An even closer look: Psalm 96

The author and the occasion on which it was written are unknown. It is immediately apparent, however, that this psalm bears a striking resemblance to a song which was composed by David (1 Chr. 16). That song was used to celebrate the Ark of the Covenant being placed in the tabernacle (2 Sam. 6:1-17; 1 Chron. 16:1).

The subscription in the Greek translation of the Old Testament (the Septuagint) associates Psalm 96 with the dedication of the rebuilt temple after the Jews returned from captivity in Babylon.

It is entirely conceivable that the original song written by David was used with some changes for this significant occasion.

The psalm finds its way into the 'enthronement' category by virtue of its ringing affirmation of the Lord's reign (v. 10) and its declarations of the greatness and majesty of the Lord (vv. 4-6).

The mighty reign of the majestic God serves here as the 'launching pad' for the author to call his people to both worship and witness.

The people of God are at their best when their worship is robust and enthusiastic and when their witness is clear and contagious. But, sadly enough, our worship is often weak and stunted and our witness often muted. This psalm consists of a fervent call to these twin responsibilities.

The call to worship (vv. 1-9)

A fervent call (v. 1)

The psalm begins with the little word 'Oh', a word that conveys great depth of feeling. Someone has observed that true Christianity always has an 'oh' in it, a sense that it is far above us and too great for us.

An instructive call (vv. 1-2,7-9)

The psalm proceeds to lay before us some of the key elements of worship. In other words, it doesn't leave us to define worship for ourselves. It tells us the following:

WORSHIP IS OWED TO GOD AND TO BE DIRECTED TO HIM (V. 1) The phrase 'all the earth' indicates that worship is a universal obligation. Even those who do not worship are under this obligation.

The recurring phrase 'to the LORD' reminds us that worship is to be directed to God (vv. 1-2,7-8). It would seem to go without saying that God is the object of worship, but we have constantly to be reminded of this because we have the tendency to shift the focus of worship to ourselves. We very easily fall into the trap of being religious consumers who attend services with the idea that something must be done for us instead of our being responsible for doing something for God.

WORSHIP IS TO BE GLAD AND OPENLY EXPRESSED (VV. 1-2,7-8) Three times the psalmist uses the word 'sing' (vv. 1-2). We associate singing with gladness of heart, but worship is not to remain in the heart. It is to come out of the mouth! The same truths are brought out by the word 'give' (vv. 7-8) which refers to the giving of praise to God.

WORSHIP IS TO BE NEW (V. 1) This doesn't mean we cannot use the same songs or words we have used before in worship, but rather these songs and words should spring from hearts that have gone anew over the greatness of our God and the salvation he has provided. Worship is to spring from hearts that are fresh with the wonder and glory of it all.

WORSHIP IS TO BE PUBLIC (V. 8) The phrase '… into his courts' brings us to the public aspect of worship. The people were to do their singing and giving praise in the place designated for worship. Private worship is necessary, but it can't replace public worship.

WORSHIP IS TO BE IN THE BEAUTY OF HOLINESS (V. 9) Matthew Henry says: 'We must worship him with holy hearts, sanctified by the grace of God, devoted to the glory of God, and purified from the pollution of sin.'[1]

WORSHIP IS TO BE REVERENT (V. 9) We are to worship with a sense of awe that is born from realizing who God is. Those who ridicule reverence in worship only give evidence that they are not duly impressed with the God with whom we have to do.

Reasons for this kind of worship are sprinkled throughout the first nine verses: God is great (v. 4), he alone is God (vv. 4-5), he is the creator of all things (v. 5), heaven is filled with his majesty and splendour (v. 6) and his sanctuary is filled with his strength and beauty (v. 6). With the last of these reasons, the psalmist may have been asserting that the temple was a holy place that reflected the strength and beauty of God. Our own worship services ought to display the same.

The call to witness (vv. 2-3,10-13)

The theme of witness is present in the first nine verses, being intertwined with the theme of worship. It is in those words 'proclaim' (v. 2) and 'declare' (v. 3).

What is to be proclaimed? The good news of God's salvation! (v. 2). This is such good news that it cannot be worn out. So our proclamation should never be worn out! It is to be 'from day to day' or day after day.

What is to be declared? The glory of the Lord! And his wonders! (v. 3). The wonders are those works that are awe-inspiring and breathtaking. And Israel's history was filled with such. Moses at the burning bush, the plagues upon Egypt, the crossing of the Red Sea, the giving of the law at Mount Sinai, the conquest of Jericho are a few of the wonders of which the people of Israel could and should speak! A glorious God can do wonders!

> What is to be proclaimed? The good news of God's salvation! (v. 2). This is such good news that it cannot be worn out. So our proclamation should never be worn out!

Wonderful as those wonders were, they do not begin to compare to the greatest wonder of all, that wonder of which all the people of God in every era can speak. This is the wonder which the psalmist has already mentioned—the wonder of salvation. It is a wonder of his grace. It consists of nothing less than the holy God making a way for his enemies to be restored to peace with himself. It is a wonder of his faithfulness. The provision of salvation fulfilled all the promises God had made throughout the Old Testament. It is a wonder of his wisdom. How could a holy God both carry out the sentence of his wrath against sinners and let those same sinners go free? God's wisdom found the way, and that way was Jesus, who received on the cross the penalty of God's wrath. Because he received it and because God only demands that the penalty for sinners be paid once, there is no penalty left for believing sinners to pay. God's salvation is the triumph of his grace, his faithfulness, his justice and his wisdom.

The emphasis on witness becomes even more apparent and sustained in the last four verses of the psalm. God's people are to declare this message to the nations: 'The LORD reigns!' (v. 10). One evidence of this is the earth itself which he has 'firmly established'.

Those who may be inclined to doubt the reign of the Lord will eventually have all the evidence they need. The very reign they question will become crystal clear when God 'shall judge the peoples righteously' (v. 10).

Another evidence of the reign of God is to be found in the one who 'is coming' (v. 13). It seems likely that the psalmist was here lifting his eyes to look towards the arrival of the Messiah. His public ministry itself would constitute a judgement upon 'the earth' (v. 13). It put the righteousness and truth of God on display for people either to accept or reject. Those who reject it will find that the righteousness and truth of Jesus will be the standard by which they will be judged when he at last comes again (Acts 17:31).

The reign of God is not, then, something to be debated and disputed. It is rather to be seen as the truth. It is a truth of such momentous importance that the entire universe should greet it with joy and gladness. And truth is not a treasure to be hoarded but good news to be shared.

FOR FURTHER STUDY

1. Read 1 Chronicles 16. Describe David's worship on this occasion.
2. Read Psalm 122. What does this psalm teach about worship?

TO THINK ABOUT AND DISCUSS

1. What can you do to improve your worship of God?
2. What can you do to improve your witness for God?

End notes

Introduction

1 *The Open Bible*, Thomas Nelson Publishers, p.538.

2 Roger Ellsworth, *The Bible Book by Book,* Evangelical Press, p.148.

3 John R.W. Stott, *Favorite Psalms*, Moody Press, p.5.

4 William Hendriksen, *Survey of the Bible*, Baker Book House, p.281.

5 Holman Bible Dictionary, Trent C. Butler, Editor, 'Book of Psalms', Broadman & Holman, p.1149.

Chapter 1

1 *Holman Bible Dictionary*, p.1150.

2 Cited by Warren W. Wiersbe, *Wiersbe's Expository Outlines on the Old Testament*, Victor Books, p.456

Chapter 3

1 Steven J. Lawson, *Holman Old Testament Commentary: Psalms 1-75*, Holman Reference, p.33.

2 Michael Wilcock, *The Bible Speaks Today: The Message of Psalms 1-72*, InterVarsity Press, p.28.

3 Lawson, p.64.

4 Cited by Joel C. Gregory, *Growing Pains*

of the Soul, Word Books, p.66.

5 Matthew Henry, *Commentary*, vol. iii, p.589.

Chapter 4

1 Peter Jeffery, *Following the Shepherd*, Evangelical Press of Wales, p.105.

2 Jeffery, p.55.

3 Matthew Henry, *Matthew Henry's Commentary*, Fleming H. Revell Company, vol. iii, p.318.

4 Henry T. Mahan, *With New Testament Eyes*, Evangelical Press, vol.i, pp.18-19.

5 Henry, vol. iii, p.318.

6 As above.

7 As above.

8 John R.W. Stott, *Favorite Psalms*, Moody Press, p.32.

Chapter 7

1 Lawson, *Holman Old Testament Commentary: Psalms 1-75*, p.29.

2 Charles Spurgeon, *The Treasury of David*, MacDonald Publishing Company, vol. i, p.24.

Chapter 9

1 see also Roger Ellsworth, *The Shepherd King*, Evangelical Press, pp.185-93.

2 Spurgeon, *Treasury*, vol. ii, p. 29.

3 As above, p. 30.

4 see also Roger Ellsworth, *The Guide to Christian Comfort*, Evangelical Press, pp.160-7.

Chaper 11

1 Albert Barnes, *Notes on the Old Testament: Psalms*, Baker Books, vol.i, p.277.

2 Matthew Henry, *Matthew Henry's Commentary*, Fleming H. Revell Publishing Company, vol, iii, p.356.

3 Spurgeon, vol.i, p.124.

4 As above, p.127.

Chapter 13

1 Stott, *Favorite Psalms*, p.68.

2 As above.

3 Barnes, *Notes*, vol.iii, p.165.

4 As above, p.166.

5 Cited in Michael Wilcock, *The Messages of Psalms 1-72*, Inter-Varsity Press, p.175.

6 Elizabeth C. Clephane, *Beneath the cross of Jesus*.

7 James Montgomery Boice, *Psalms*,

Baker Books, vol. iii, p.949.

8 Barnes, *Notes*, vol.iii, p.167.

Chapter 14

1 Henry, *Commentary*, vol. iii, p.779.

2 Barnes, *Notes*, vol. iii, p.330.

Chapter 15

1 Henry, *Commentary*, vol. iii, p.756.

2 As above, p.758.

3 Barnes, *Notes*, vol. iii. p.339.

4 Stott, *Favorite Psalms*, p.125.

5 As above, p.127.

Chapter 16

1 Henry T. Mahan, *With New Testament Eyes*, Evangelical Press, vol. ii, p.52.

Chapter 17

1 Barnes, *Notes*, vol. i, p.313.

2 As above, p.314.

Chapter 18

1 Henry, *Commentary*, vol. iii, p.633.

2 As above, p.634.

Chapter 19

1 *The Open Bible*, p.539.

2 J.I. Packer, *God Speaks to Man*, The Westminster Press, p.75.

3 As above, p.76.

4 Harry Mennega, cited by James E. Adams, *War Psalms of the Prince of Peace*, Presbyterian and Reformed Publishing Company, p.50.

5 Johannes G. Vos, as above.

6 As above, p.111.

7 Michael Wilcock, (vol. i, p.209)

8 , Henry, *Commentary*, vol. iii, p.452.

Chapter 20

1 Henry, *Commentary*, vol. iii, p.554.

2 Barnes, *Notes*, vol. ii, p.337.

3 Henry, *Commentary*, vol. iii, p.555.

Chapter 21

1 cited by Spurgeon, *Treasury*, vol. i, p.305.

2 As above, p.303.

Chapter 23

1 Spurgeon, *Treasury*, vol. i, p.11.

2 quoted by Spurgeon, *Treasury*, vol. i, p.12.

3 Henry, *Commentary*, vol. iii, p.658.

4 Barnes, *Notes*, vol. iii, p.136.

5 Walter Chantry, *Praises for the King of Kings*, The Banner of Truth Trust, p.64.

6 Barnes, *Notes*, vol. iii, p.138.

Chapter 24

1 Roger Ellsworth, *Journey to the Cross*, Evangelical Press, pp.55-60.

2 *New Geneva Study Bible: New King James Version*, Thomas Nelson Publishers, p.776.

Chapter 25

1 Derek Kidner, *Psalms 1-72*, Inter-Varsity Press, p.177.

2 Barnes, *Notes*, vol. ii, p.48.

3 As above, vol.iii, p.26.

Chapter 26

1 Henry, *Commentary*, vol.iii, pp.604-5.

223

The
Opening
up
series

Opening up
Exodus

Opening up
Ezra

Opening up
Psalms

Opening up
Ecclesiastes

Opening up
Ezekiel's visions

Opening up
Amos

Opening up
Nahum

Opening up
1 Corinthians

Further
titles in
preparation

Opening up
Philippians

Opening up
1 Thessalonians

Opening up
1 Timothy

Opening up
2 & 3 John

This fine series is aimed at the 'average person in the church' and combines brevity, accuracy and readability with an attractive page layout. Thought-provoking questions make the books ideal for both personal or small group use.

'Laden with insightful quotes and penetrating practical application, Opening up Philippians is a Bible study tool which belongs on every Christian's bookshelf!'

DR. PHIL ROBERTS, PRESIDENT, MIDWESTERN BAPTIST THEOLOGICAL SEMINARY, KANSAS CITY, M I S S O U R I

Please contact us for a free catalogue

In the UK ☎ 01568 613 740   **email—** sales@dayone.co.uk

In the United States: ☎ Toll Free:1-8-morebooks

In Canada: ☎ 519 763 0339 www.dayone.co.uk